# THE NEW SUPERVISOR

**SECOND EDITION**

MARTIN M. BROADWELL
Training Consultant

# THE NEW SUPERVISOR

**SECOND EDITION**

ADDISON-WESLEY PUBLISHING COMPANY
Reading, Massachusetts · Menlo Park, California
London · Amsterdam · Don Mills, Ontario · Sydney

**Library of Congress Cataloging in Publication Data**

Broadwell, Martin M
    The new supervisor.

    Includes index.
    1. Supervision of employees.    I.    Title.
HF5549.B855  1979         658.3'02         78-73365
ISBN 0-201-00565-4

ISBN 0-201-00565-4
CDEFGHIJK-AL-8987654321

To the men in my life:
*My father*
*My brother*
*My two sons*

# PREFACE TO
# THE SECOND EDITION

Since the first edition of this book was published, many new supervisors have come into the work force. Most made it very well without ever knowing this book existed. Some knew of it and even read some in it. One thing we can say for certain: None who made it to the ranks of new supervisors did so without having to learn some of the things contained in this little volume.

The intent of the revision that led to the second edition was not only to update the book but also to fill in some of the holes that invariably show up when a book first comes out. One thing that has been added to enhance the use of this book as a training device is an exercise section at the end of each chapter. These discussions and activities will allow the reader to study the book as a part of group exercise or go through it alone and ponder the questions asked.

Another addition is the section in Chapter 9 on the employment interview. This section seemed necessary because of problems arising from misunderstanding and lack of knowledge of the antidiscrimination laws that have come into effect in the recent years. It was felt that a separate section would: (1) serve as a handy, unified reference to the subject, and (2) allow us to deal directly with the questions that would be raised, rather than to work them into the rest of the chapter on interviewing. Hopefully, the reader will also check with his or her own organization for further clarification on this important matter.

Another part of the revision has to do with adding some words about "production-minded management" in Chapter 8. In the last few years, words like "profit" and "savings" and "production" have come back into vogue, and are no longer considered a forbidden part of the supervisor's vocabulary. This doesn't change the basic things we know or should be doing in supervision, but does broaden our scope of operational thought a bit!

Finally, in the chapter on training (Chapter 10) there is some information on how to do effective *classroom training*. More and more, organizations are calling on their experienced supervisors—and this often means the newly appointed ones—to provide classroom instruction in their field of expertise. Some of the hints and helps should make the task easier and perhaps even more fun. And speaking of fun, since this book first came out, nothing has happened to make supervision any less fun. True, there are things that make it even more challenging, but with a little luck, a little knowledge, and a lot of fortitude, the new supervisor can make his or her way right along the path to satisfaction and pleasure in the job. Many have and continue to do so every day. So can you!

*Decatur, Georgia*                                                                    M. M. B.
*January 1979*

# ACKNOWLEDGEMENTS

Anyone who reads a book may say, "My, how smart the author is!" Anyone who writes a book must say, "I hope no one ever realizes how much of this I got from someone else!" Let the reader of this book know that the author doesn't ask those who have contributed so much to it to accept the blame for the way it came out, only to take credit for heading him in the right direction. In this book each will recognize the part that once was his idea, his manner of expressing the old thing in a new way, or making the new idea sound not too far out:

*Cabot Jaffee*
*Dugan Laird*
*Brother Bill*
*Dick Grote*
and *John Sajem,* whose steady hand makes the pictures flow so well!

M. M. B.

# CONTENTS

# PROLOGUE

All the books in the world won't prepare a person adequately for that first day—or even the first few weeks—as a supervisor. The first time we have responsibility not only for the job but also for the people doing the job, it can be an awesome thing. But the job becomes rewarding when it is done properly, and it can be done that way if we avoid certain mistakes.

The purpose of this book is to help keep the new supervisor from doing wrong some things that others did wrong when they became new supervisors. There is very little theory in this book, but that isn't to say that practical application of many theories isn't here. People do not act theoretically; neither can they be supervised theoretically. The new supervisor has gone too far to be satisfied with just theories, no matter how good they are or how practical they have proven to be. What he or she wants to know is "What do I do right now with *this* problem?"

Hopefully this book will help answer that question.

# 1
# A NEW ATTITUDE TOWARD THE JOB

## A NEW ROLE

Supervising others can be fully understood only by those who do it. This doesn't mean it is mysterious or deep, it just means it's hard to explain—like describing chocolate cake to someone who has never eaten cake. That first day on the job can be frustrating, and many supervisors have been heard to say, "I didn't know how well off I was. At least I knew what I was doing." And therein lies the problem. When we become supervisors, we must realize that we've taken on a new role, one for which we have the qualifications—but for which we *probably haven't been trained.*

There was one thing about the old job—we knew what to do and when to do it. In fact, that's probably why we got our new job in the first place; we could do our job better than anyone else. Someone looked at us and decided we were pretty good at our job and seemed to have the qualities for making a good supervisor. So they promoted us to supervisor. Now we have the job, but what do we do? In the old job we were trained. We were never given a job to do and left with no more instruction than "Just do what comes naturally to you." But that's the situation right now. We have people working for us and we really can't do their work for them. Our job is to see that *they* do the work. No matter how slow they seem to be, or how bad their attitude may be, or how much they foul up the job, our role is still to get work done by them, *not do it ourselves.*

Remember when we used to gripe about the boss doing things wrong? Remember those sessions around the coffee pot when we and the rest of the workers used to really let the boss have it (behind his or her back, of course)? Well, we're the bosses now, and they're talking about us around the coffee pot. This means we are going to have to start looking at things differently. *Our job is to worry about the job.* This doesn't mean our people aren't important—we've already seen that they are the ones who do the work for us—but it means that we must learn to think about both the people and the job, not letting either one get more important than the other. And that's pretty difficult, as we will see time and again in this book.

Let's look at a simple example: Susan comes in red-eyed and obviously has a problem. As the story unfolds, it looks something like this:

> Susan's having family problems. She and her husband haven't been married very long and this morning they had an argument. The husband was pretty hateful and said some pretty mean things. Susan has decided to go home to Mother, and wants to take the afternoon off so she can go home and pack before her husband gets there. The only thing is, she can't afford to lose the pay (now that she's on her own) and wants to come in on a Saturday and make it up. This means actually showing her time as worked this afternoon, but nothing on the Saturday she works. She is willing to work all day for the halftime off so as not to lose the money. The truth is, we can't afford to let her go—even without pay—because of the heavy work load today. But as distraught as she is, there's no telling how she will react if we tell her she can't go. Also, if we say no, she'll think it's just because we weren't willing to let her make it up on a Saturday. She's waiting now for an answer and needs it immediately so she can call her mother.

Well, *what do we do?* The problem is real and important to Susan. As supervisors, we are expected to make the right decisions. Suppose we let her go, with or without pay; what will we tell Swinging Sally when she comes in next Friday to do the same thing so she can go to Daytona Beach with the guys for spring vacation? How will we explain to her the difference in our treatment of the two situations? Suppose we don't let her go; how much production can we expect to get out of her for the rest of the day? How will we explain the loss in production to our boss? What will our decision do to the morale in the office? Does it matter?

## NEW WORDS—NEW MEANINGS TO OLD ONES

As we go along we will see better approaches to solving this kind of problem than just doing what comes naturally. But for now, let's say that we must learn a new vocabulary. At least, we must learn new meanings for old words. They are going to be key words and key meanings for years to come. They are going to be the things that we spend our time thinking about, worrying about, and making decisions about. Words like *management* take on a different look now. Also *money* and *time* aren't bad words anymore. We can't make decisions just on the basis of emotions, or even on the feelings of the people involved. We make the decisions on the basis of good job management. We make them in light of what's good for the organization—which *includes the feelings* of the people but not *only* the feelings of the people.

All of this says that the word "production" should take on a new meaning for us. We aren't responsible just for things anymore; people and money and time and production have suddenly become inseparable. And remember, the thing we were the best at—getting the job done— we no longer are supposed to do (at least not with our hands). And remember, too, we may not have been trained to do this new job of supervising people. Of course, there are some basic rules: treat them as we would like to be treated; remember that they are human beings— the basic human courtesies still apply. But we may not even be sure how we would like to be treated in a similar situation. Also, knowing what we do about production needs and work scheduling and profits and the bosses' demands means that we would want to be treated differently from those who don't know about these things. And suppose we decide that Susan and Sally *are* human beings—so what? That's a nice thought, but what do we do with their problems now that they've become human beings? What do we do about getting the job done?

Though this may sound a bit heartless, it really isn't. It just means that being a supervisor changes things for us. It changes our outlook and presents us with new problems. It changes our perspective and gives us a bigger picture to look at. It doesn't take the human element out; it puts other elements in. It gives us more factors to consider when we make decisions. It does, in fact, give us the right and opportunity to make decisions that were not ours to make before. As we said before, the *job* becomes important now, and all these other things are part of getting the job done. It doesn't make us any less interested in people; it makes us interested in people even more, but in a different way. We are interested in them because they are the ones that make us look good or bad. They have been entrusted—in a sense—into our hands, and we have an obligation to see that things go well for them. But the job has been entrusted to us, also, and we have an obligation to the organization to see that the work is done so that *all concerned* will profit.

## A DIFFERENT GANG NOW

The supervisory role has been referred to as the lonely role. It looked simple enough when we were working for the boss and he or she was making all the decisions. It didn't seem too bad when he or she just seemed to hang around doing very little but getting in the way. As a matter of fact, we remember when we used to say, "Boy, that's really having it made. We do all the work and the boss gets the credit and the money and the office!" This job looked pretty easy when we were the Susans and Jims. But somehow it doesn't look now the way it did then. Susan and Sally and Jim and Chuck even look different to us now. But they haven't changed. And we haven't changed. So what's different? The *job* is different. The responsibility has changed. Our viewpoint has changed. And let's face it, our loyalties have probably changed, too. Whether we like it or not, the people working for us don't see us the same way now that we are the boss. And we really can't afford to see them the same way, either. A few supervisors have been able to make a go of it by telling the old gang that nothing has changed. They have continued to go on break and eat lunch with them and gripe with them and criticize the organization with them, and knock the big boss with them and still get the work done and handle discipline problems and fire some and promote some and not get into trouble with the group—but there aren't many successes who took this route, and there are plenty of failures to show that it is a dangerous route to take. Being a regular guy is nice, and it's all right, too—but only if the phrase means that even though you are the *boss,* you're still a regular guy. You can't give up being the boss just to stay a regular guy.

The important thing is that we belong to a different gang now. We have to give up some of the pleasures of being part of the old gang and accept our position as the boss. As the boss, we belong to the gang that is made up of the other bosses. We don't have to associate with them, but we have to communicate with them, on their level (which is our level, too). We still have to communicate with those who work for us, and on their level, too (which is *not* our level). As we look out over the group that works for us, we must say, "We are a group that must stick together, perform as one unit and meet the organization's goals. But even though we work as one, I must be the leader. I must set the pattern of leadership by letting them be a part of the goal-setting; I must lead by giving them as much authority as possible so they can do their job with a minimum of interference from me; I must see that they develop their full potential; I must see that their needs are met; *but*—I must do these things as the boss, not as just one of them."

How do we accomplish this without being snobbish or conceited or overbearing? It isn't easy, but it isn't impossible. In the next chapter we will see some examples of how it can be done successfully.

## CONCLUSION

The role of a new supervisor is quite a change from whatever else we have been doing. Coming from within the organization will cause one kind of problem, coming from outside will cause another. In either case, though, things are going to be different from now on. The *purpose* of the job is different. Viewpoints are different. Like it or not, we're part of a different group now; we're part of the managing effort, rather than a part of the hourly worker effort. Our job is now to get the work done through others, not do it ourselves. Instead of griping about the boss, we're the boss. Instead of griping about policy, we're the ones who must implement the policy. Instead of just waiting for someone to appraise us, we must do appraisals of others. This goes on and on, because we've taken on this new role. It takes some getting used to, but we can do it. Many have before us, and they're better for it. We will be, too!

## EXERCISES

1. Individual activity: Let each person write down how he or she got to be a supervisor. (What do they think the processes were—in the minds of the decision makers—that led to the promotion?) Even if the person was *hired* into the organization as a supervisor, what led the organization to choose this person over another—as a *supervisor*?

2. Half-group activity: Divide the group into two subgroups. Have one subgroup list what might be typical viewpoints of hourly workers toward the job of supervision, and the other subgroup list how a newly appointed supervisor might feel about supervision the first week after taking the job. Record the lists in separate places.

3. From the above lists, let each person vote "Agree" or "Disagree" on each item in each list. Do the majority of the group members agree with the hourly workers or with the supervisors?

4. Group discussion: In a group discussion, come up with a list of things that ought to be taken into consideration in selecting a person for the job of supervisor. Let the whole group get agreement on as many things as possible. (The dissenters should be answered by those who are in favor of the item under discussion.)

5. Small-group activity: Working in several small groups, give the subgroups two or three of the items from number 4 and have each decide how their items could be measured. (Be sure that each item is measured well enough—by their suggestions—so that each person's work can be distinguished from that of the others.)

6. Half-group activity: Divide the group into two subgroups. Have one group represent typical hourly workers and the other group represent typical first-line supervisors. Have them look at the following words and give their "feelings" about each of them. After each individual does this, each subgroup should try to come up with a consensus on each word. In discussing them afterward, see if there is even a difference in the definition in the words themselves. The words to be discussed are:

| | | |
|---|---|---|
| Time off | Money | Production |
| Management | Work | Overtime |
| Profit | The boss | Union |

# 2
# A NEW ATTITUDE
# TOWARD THE SUBORDINATE

As new supervisors, one of the most difficult things for us to accept is
the fact that those under us might be able to do our job just as well as
we can do it. In fact, in different circumstances, one of those under us
might well have been the boss instead of us. What made the difference?
Brain power? Probably not. In sheer ability to think, most of us come
out very close to the middle range, even though we like to think of it
otherwise. The fact that we are bosses doesn't reduce the brain power
of those we supervise, or mean that we necessarily have more than they
have. What about knowledge of the job? This varies, of course, because
many new supervisors know their former job better than anyone else
(which may well be the reason they were selected for the supervisory
job in the first place). On the other hand, as new supervisors, we may
know less about the job we're supervising than anyone else (having been
promoted from some other job, or hired into the supervisory job). Over-
looking the matter of luck or influence, the only thing we can say for
sure is that the new supervisor gets the job because somebody in higher
management thinks he or she can handle the job of getting work done
by directing the activities of others.

## RECOGNIZE THEIR ABILITIES

So what, then, should be our attitude toward those who work for us?
The important thing to remember is that it is to our—and the company's—advantage to use their talents as much as possible, leaving less
and less of their job for us to do! It's rather poor management of time,
people, and talent to let brainpower go unused, or to let experience and
knowledge of the job be wasted. And the chances are pretty good that
our people will use these things or not use them *as a result of things
that we do or don't do.* In a sense we can think of our people as being
a huge storehouse of brainpower and knowledge of the job. The only

catch is that we must find the right keys to give us access to this tremendous asset. Not every key will work every time, nor will every key work on every individual. We spend much of our time looking for the right keys and trying them out when we find them. (All of which adds to the fun and challenge of being a supervisor!)

## SUBORDINATES HAVE NEEDS

Those who work for us have more than brainpower, job knowledge, and experience—they have certain needs and anxieties that work against them for awhile, but can be made to work for us. For example, if their needs are being met on the job, then we have found a good source of motivation. On the other hand, if the needs are very strong and are *not* being met on the job, then no matter how hard we work at motivating, we aren't likely to have much success. It isn't enough to just say, "Well, I have problems, too, and I don't let it influence my performance." That may or may not be true, but in any case, we still have to recognize the problems that the employee brings to work with him. This doesn't mean we have to excuse poor performance caused by outside problems, but it does mean we have to accept the fact that the employee has those problems and that they may affect his work.

But outside problems aren't the only things that cause employees to have anxieties; there are many things right on the job that will bother them and cause them to develop additional problems. For example, just the fact that you're new to the job as supervisor will cause certain anxieties. The employees don't know how they will relate to you. They don't know how they will fit into your thinking. They will worry about your opinion of them and the impression you will get of their work. They will have to start all over again competing with the others in the organization to establish a position in your esteem. These aren't necessarily large problems, but they are real and must be considered by the new supervisor.

Not only will employees worry about how you will see them but they will also be watching you to see how you act under certain conditions. What will it be like when there is a rush job to be done? Will you be the kind that puts the screws on tight, or will you just relax and not worry about deadlines? What happens when an employee does something wrong? Will you be tolerant and just say, "Forget it"? Or will you blow your stack and embarrass him or her in front of everyone? What happens when other departments or groups interfere with your activities, or don't meet their deadlines? Will you stand up for your "rights," or will you let them run all over you? Your employees want to know these things about you and will be anxious about it until the questions are resolved (or until you have acted in such a way as to assure them that they don't have to worry about these things).

## AMBIVALENCE—LOVE AND HATE

One of the strange things about being a supervisor is that we have to learn that it's possible for our people to love us and hate us at the same time. Perhaps these terms are too strong, but they identify the problems brought about by the phenomenon of "ambivalence." This simply means that because we represent two different things to employees, it's possible for them to feel two different ways about us. As a supervisor, we represent authority—something that tells them what to do and what not to do, hence a threat to their satisfaction. As a supervisor, we represent employees' means of getting ahead, of getting a raise, of solving their problems, of being recognized, of being told how to do things more easily, hence real security. Just as we are simultaneously a comfort and a threat to them, so they can like us for what we do for them and dislike us for what we stand for. This shows itself in the reactions of employees to the ways in which we give them assignments. If we just make assignments and don't give the employees much direction, they complain because we haven't explained to them how we want the job done. If we give them instructions, they're apt to complain because we lean over their shoulders all the time and don't let them do anything on their own. Again, our job as a supervisor is to recognize that this phenomenon exists, and to look for ways of using it to our advantage.

## BOSSES ARE NICE PEOPLE

Often we find ourselves in the peculiar position of seeming to defend our "bosshood." Very early in the game we must realize that *there is nothing wrong with being a boss.* We should never feel the need to apologize for it or defend it. Every organization, at almost any level, must have someone who is in charge: the boss. For whatever reason, we are that person in this situation, and it's up to us to act the part. As a matter of fact, if we find ourselves trying to defend our job as the boss, we probably have a good indication that we aren't being a very good one. ("Look fellows, I hate to sound like the boss, but we've got to get this job out today.")

Interestingly enough, while we may try to hide the fact or avoid it, the employees never really get over the obvious fact that we are the boss. Whether or not we act like it is our choice; they still know we are, in spite of whatever we do. All this means is that we should get the work done by being the boss, not by trying to be a friend or a buddy, or trying to bribe the employees into doing what they are being paid to do. The problems of supervision arise not because we are the boss, but because we don't act like a boss, or perhaps because we exploit the job of being the boss. While we have every right to be the boss, we have no right to use this fact as the only means of getting the work done. We can't demand that the employees respect us, and although we can get work out for awhile by demanding it, sooner or later such action breeds disrespect that comes back to haunt us. One of the quickest haunting jobs occurs when we've acted this way for some time, then suddenly find ourselves in a situation in which it's up to the employees to pull our chestnuts out of the fire—and of course they "innocently" let these chestnuts burn! So how do we act? Later in this book we will deal with some specific behavior that has proven to be very satisfactory in setting up the right relationship between the boss and the subordinate. Right now we are just suggesting that somewhere between the two extremes of trying to hide being boss and exploiting it lies the happy ground of being successful at it.

## WE DEPEND ON OUR PEOPLE

Whether we like it or not, we still must depend on our people to accomplish the long range goals of the organization. We can do only a certain amount ourselves, and the more of the work we do the poorer job of supervision we're doing. Sooner or later we must get the work done through the people the organization has given us to do it with. That is why our attitude toward these people is so important. We may not think we have enough people, or the right people, or enough time or enough training, but it is still up to us as supervisors to get the work done with these people at this time under these conditions.

And this brings us to another critical thought: These are also the people that will make us look good or bad. These are the people who—to a large degree—can make us or break us as supervisors. Our ability to use their skills, our ability to motivate them to perform, our ability to get them to think and do the way the organization wants are the things we will be rated on when appraisal time rolls around. So their performance will have a direct and important bearing on our rating as a supervisor.

## THEY GET OUR JOB

Finally, our attitude toward our people is important because we have an obligation to the organization to see that those who work for us develop the right attitude. It is from their ranks that our job, or others like ours, must be filled, and the way we train them, use them, and treat them will determine whether or not the organization has enough properly trained supervisors to replace us and others like us when we move on to better things. Our attitude toward them may well determine the attitude they have toward their subordinates when they are promoted. Equally important, it may determine their attitude toward the organization as a whole, both right now and when they become supervisors. It is just as shortsighted to think of our people only in the jobs they fill as it is to think of ourselves as only in the job we fill. And it is certainly an indictment of us if we have failed to develop anyone under us who is capable of handling much, if not all, of our work when we are out of the office or when we are moved to another assignment.

## CONCLUSION

What have we said about our attitude toward our subordinates? We have said that we must realize that they have a storehouse of brain power and experience for which the successful supervisor will find keys. It is through the abilities of the subordinates that the job must get done. We've seen that the subordinates have certain needs and anxieties that they brought to the job or that may have developed after they got there. In fact, we are part of the problem, because we represent both a threat and a source of security to them. In the process of getting the job done, we've got to be careful not to try to defend being the boss. We don't need to defend it or hide it, but we don't want to exploit it, because the people who work for us are the means by which the organization will meet its objectives. These are the same people that will determine to a large degree just how well we do when we are appraised, because our job is really one of getting the work done through them. Finally, these are the people who should be able to move into our job when we are moved on to other jobs. Our *attitude* toward these people will largely determine our *actions* toward them; hence it will determine how well they are able to take over when we leave.

## EXERCISES

1. Group discussion: Have the group brainstorm ways in which non-supervisors or hourly workers have problems that are exactly the same as supervisors. This isn't limited just to the job activities, but includes their home life, community, future planning, money, etc. Record this and then discuss why oftentimes supervisors tend to think their people shouldn't have personal problems—or at least should not let them interfere with the job.

2. Using the list above, have the group decide whether these problems we all have in common actually *do* interfere with supervisors and their jobs.

3. Group discussion: Have the group brainstorm ways in which non-supervisors or hourly workers have problems that are *not* like those of typical supervisors. Record this and decide whether these problems interfere with work. Do supervisors let their "nonsimilar" problems interfere with their work?

4. Individual assignment: Let each person make a list of the ways "ambivalence" is displayed in the work place. Find places where the boss is criticized by the workers for doing something, but where there would also be criticism if the boss failed to do it. We discussed this in this chapter, using the example of close supervision versus not enough direction.

5. Subgroup activity: Divide the group into two subgroups. Have one subgroup think of ways in which supervisors can and should use their positions as *bosses* to their advantage. The other subgroup should think of ways and times when letting it be known that we are the boss can be harmful. One group is discussing the advantages of using the position of boss and the other is listing the disadvantages, both with specific examples.

6. Group discussion: Discuss ways in which the job couldn't get done if the workers under us decided to do just what they were told to do and *no more*. Give some specific examples.

# 3
# A NEW ATTITUDE TOWARD THE BOSS

## BOSSES HAVE THEIR OWN PROBLEMS

One of the things that confronts us soon after we become new supervisors is the fact that our problems are often compounded by our people coming in with *their* problems, which gives us less time for our own. This really ought to be a very loud message for us: If it's true for us, it must surely be true for *our* boss! In fact, it is very true. Even though we don't like to admit it sometimes, the boss is usually working on problems of greater magnitude than ours. In a sense, our problems are really our boss's too, and so are all the problems of the other people who work for him or her. Even if our boss hasn't got more important problems, he or she at least has *more*. It behooves us, then, to avoid adding our problems to our boss's burdens, or at least not adding any more than we can help.

The thing we want to do is make very sure that we understand the boss's role and our own role, and where the dividing line is between them. We need to remember that just as it's our job to get a certain portion of the work done through other people, so it is the boss's job to get things done through us. If we get the idea that the boss is just sitting around giving us work so he or she won't have anything to do, let's stop and realize that our people may feel the same way about us! Another thing we need to remember is that since our boss has the responsibility for our decisions—as well as the decisions of his or her other subordinates—any bad decisions he or she makes have more important results than ours would. This doesn't mean that we can forget about using good judgment, or that our boss is going to check everything we do anyway, so why worry about doing it right. It means just the opposite; it means that the better judgment we use, and the better job we do, the better job the boss can do. We help our boss handle the bigger, broader problems with better judgment because we have bought him or her a little more time (now that he or she doesn't have to worry about

13

our mistakes and poor judgment). And the better our boss does, the better will be the final results for us. Even if we don't get the credit for a job well done, we are still in the *group* that got the good results, and it will pay off in the long run.

## BOSSES HAVE FEELINGS TOO

Most supervisory training we will get as new supervisors will tell us that our people have feelings, anxieties, problems, needs, etc., a fact we all readily agree with. But sometimes the implication is that we as bosses *don't* have any feelings or problems, or at least that we aren't supposed to let them show. Actually no one argues that bosses don't have problems, and most will agree that we need to be careful about letting these problems affect our behavior. Even so, we have to admit that they *do* show sometimes. We can't help it, perhaps. But wait—if we admit that we have feelings that show sometimes, shouldn't we also admit that our boss must also have problems and feelings that may show in his or her behavior from time to time? As a matter of fact, our boss has just about every problem and anxiety that we might have: worries about home, family, money, chances for promotion, relationship with the others on the same level, and whether or not he or she is being a good boss. And of course, like ourselves, our boss is concerned about the relationship with his or her own boss. We're kidding ourselves if we think we have a monopoly on problems, either personal or office.

We tend to forget that the boss has a boss, too. As much as we'd like to think that our boss always worries about us first, we'd be more honest to admit that *we don't even do that for our people.* When the going gets rough around the office or shop, we can't help but think, "How's this going to affect me?" We don't start to worry about those under us until after we've answered that question. So it is with most bosses, including our own, most likely. But that's all right, as long as we recognize that our boss is only acting human, and is reacting about the same way we would under similar circumstances. That's no excuse for our boss to treat his or her people wrongly in such situations, but at least we recognize the reason for the behavior and so may know how to act in return.

## THE BOSS IS ONE STEP REMOVED

One problem that confronts our boss is that of being one step removed from the job and activity of our people, just as we're one step removed from our boss's boss. This means there's a chance our boss is not getting a full view of the situation, just as we may not be seeing things from the same angle as he or she does up the line. The chances are pretty good that our boss won't see things the same way we see them, especially about our people and their work. Our boss must see all of this through the information we provide and from personal observation, then relate it to the bigger organizational picture he or she is looking at. Also, our boss has certain charges from his or her boss, certain objectives that he or she has set, and other people to worry about besides us and our people—all of which cause him or her to see things quite differently from the way we do. So there shouldn't be any great mystery if our boss's interpretation of these things differs from ours.

Take the matter of appraising our people. Being one step removed, our boss may fail to see the potential we see in some of our people. He or she may be judging them on past performance and fail to realize how well they are developing. Since we see them every day, we have a much better chance to see how they develop and how much better they handle responsibility than they did a few weeks ago. Our boss's opinion of the person we have in mind may be based on past performance that created an unfavorable impression, so our boss can't believe that there has been a change. By the same token, our boss may find it hard to believe that a person isn't performing as well as he or she should be. We may have an employee who was rated as satisfactory at one time but for some reason is just not performing up to the standard we expect.

Our boss may be dubious about our evaluation because the previous record doesn't bear us out. To make matters worse, since he or she must base a judgment on less information than we have, our boss may form opinions on incorrect information or even for emotional reasons. He or she may base an opinion on something overheard on the elevator or something heard about the employee through someone else. While such information is not reliable, it may be all that our boss has, especially if we have failed to keep him or her properly informed. We all form opinions based on the information we have to work with—the boss is no exception.

## WE ARE ONE STEP REMOVED, TOO

The boss isn't the only one who is apt to form opinions on limited amounts of information. We, too, are oftentimes guilty. We must be careful not to pass judgment on policies too quickly, before getting the whole story. Policies that are set one or more steps above our boss will likely lose some of their meaning and reason for existence by the time they get to us. Not only that, but the boss sees them in relation to his or her job and subordinates; we see them in relation to *our* job and subordinates. Each of us has a particular window to look out of, so each sees something a little different from what the other sees.

Policies that are not fully explained may appear to be unreasonable. When we fail to get the whole picture, we may say that the organization is making bad decisions. If we don't know all the facts, we just don't see things as we should. Does this mean that the boss ought to tell us everything he or she knows and the reasoning behind every decision that is made? Of course not, although we often act as though we expect it. At some point we need to develop enough confidence in the boss and the organization to realize that they are making decisions on the basis of more and better information than we have. If we still have some doubts, then we should try to find out more about the reasons behind what is happening. This is the place to *request* the information, though, not *demand* it. The boss is obligated to help us as much as possible, but not to spend all his or her time trying to justify everything the organization does. We ought to realize that we wouldn't want our people using up our time in this manner. We don't mind explaining; in fact we should make an effort to tell as much as we can about the rationale behind policies. But this doesn't mean that the only way to motivate our employees is to spend most of our time defending and justifying the organization's policies.

One problem we have as a new supervisor is that we are sort of starting from scratch in finding out just what the organization's goals really are. Because we are new, we naturally are missing quite a bit of background on why the organization does certain things in certain ways. This will work a hardship on us because we may find ourselves going off in the wrong direction without even realizing it, then having to reverse ourselves and perhaps lose face in doing so. There aren't many orientation programs that will bring us up to date on all the things we need to know about the background of the group, the department, and the organization as a whole—so we must hit the ground running in order to catch up. We can't just sit back and say, "Well, now that I'm a supervisor, it's up to the organization to train me in all the things I need to know." When we accepted the job as supervisor, we also accepted the responsibility for a large amount of our own development, including finding out about how and why things are run the way they are. The task is a difficult one, but it must be accomplished if we are to make a success of the new job.

## CONCLUSION

As new supervisors, we must develop the proper attitude toward our boss and his or her job. We must recognize that our boss has to worry not only about us and our job, but also about the others working for him or her. At the same time, our boss is human and will have many of the same problems and anxieties that we have, and they may show on the job. He or she also works for someone else, and so is likely to worry some about his or her own position in the organization. And since our boss is one step removed from our people and their work, he or she gets much less information about our people than we do, and so may reach different or even wrong conclusions about which of our people are good and which are doing well on the job. At the same time, we are one step removed from our boss's supervisors, so we may get the wrong impressions about the policies and decisions that are made at their level. We can't expect our boss to explain every detail and every reason for every act, so we must develop confidence in those who make the policies and ask about only those things we need to know more about in order to explain to our people. Finally, we will find it hard to learn all that we need to know about the background of the organization and its people when we first make supervisor. While the organization should provide as much training as possible, the responsibility is still ours to do as much self-development as possible. Because there is so much to be learned and not much time to learn it, a good relationship with our boss will go a long way toward building mutual confidence to sustain us across the gaps in our knowledge.

## EXERCISES

1. Small-group activity: Break the group into several small groups, and have them discuss and list ways in which we cause our bosses problems without even realizing it sometimes. Don't just think of it in terms of one person working for another; rather think in terms of a first-line supervisor working for the next level of supervision. This information should then be shared with the entire group with a discussion of how these things could be avoided.

2. Small-group activity: In the same small groups, make a list of ways the next level of supervision makes problems for the first line of supervision, without realizing it. Again, discuss ways in which this could be overcome.

3. Group discussion: Come up with a list of problems the second level of supervision has—in being the boss—that the first line of supervision does not have. Remember, the second level of supervision has problems that are *people* problems, too. In many ways there are similarities, but in some ways there are differences. List not only the people problems, though; think in terms of organization problems, too. These should be recorded and kept for further discussion.

4. Small-group activity: Have small groups discuss certain of those problems discovered in exercise 3 above, with the idea of finding ways the first level could make life easier for the next level. What could we do at first level to ease some of the problems listed here?

5. Group discussion: Communicating up and down the line in any organization is always a problem. The first level of supervision is at the bottom of the ladder as far as the management is concerned. This means that they will often be the last to get information about policy, reorganization, problems, and goals. The group should generate a list of things that are likely not to get to the first line of supervision until after they've been implemented—and maybe not until they've begun to affect the organization. The idea is to look for things that happen or are decided upon that actually go into effect before the lowest level of supervision finds out about it in

the *normal* operation of the business. For example, the budget is set, promotions are made, there is a reorganization at top level, etc. List these things for later discussion.

6. Half-group activity: Divide the group into two subgroups. Have one half of the group debate the other on each of the items above, one side taking the position that there is no reason for sharing this information with the first-line people before going ahead, and the other taking the position that it is essential that first-line people be aware of the proposed changes or other decisions before they become a part of the organization's activity.

# 4

# SUPERVISORS' RELATIONS WITH THEIR COORDINATES

## GROWING UP IS ESSENTIAL

It sometimes surprises new supervisors that there is so much bickering and infighting going on among the other supervisors—their coordinates. If we're smart, we'll react by saying to ourselves, "Why don't they grow up?" That's the real problem. The ability to get along in a work situation where everyone has the same general working conditions, the same boss, and the same organizational policies to work with, is a measure of our maturity. It all seems pretty ridiculous, because most of us would rather work in a situation where everyone got along with everyone else, where everyone did their job and nobody complained about anything. But that's a dream world that just doesn't exist. Do we just give in, then, and prepare for battle?

Not if we want to get our job done and help the organization toward its goals. The thing that is important is that all of our ultimate goals are the same (or should be). We want the organization to prosper; goals to be met; more money to be made available (through our efficient use of what we have) so that there will be raises and promotions. The problem is that while we may have the same long-range goals, the short-range ones seem to differ—even to be opposed to one another. Each supervisor is assigned a task, people to do that task, money to carry out the job, etc. Each task seems different in its purpose and goals. So conflict soon arises. We each become intent on reaching *our* goal with *our* money and *our* people. Each of us has his or her own problems to solve and own means of solving them. The conflict arises when we get so intent on our *own* problems that we lose sight of the organization's goals and problems. We resent anyone that seems to get in our way while we are striving to get where the organization wants us to go. We forget that the organization wants us to get there *together* with the other supervisors, not with their bodies strewn out behind us!

## GET THE JOB DONE, BUT . . .

Sooner or later, someone will emerge as the leader of a "Let's-get-along" movement. Why shouldn't it be us? We can do our part in seeing that things run smoothly and still get the job done. We really don't have many choices in our relationships with our coordinates. We can get the job done by walking all over them, caring little for how they look or feel. Or we can get our job done by issuing edicts like, "Forget about them, let's get the job done." In other words, we can just ignore the supervisors we are supposed to be working with. Or, finally, we can get the job done through a cooperative effort, taking everything into consideration. When we think about how ridiculous it is to spend our time bickering, it's easy to see that the last alternative is the only practical one. To get the job done over the dead bodies of the ones we should be working with will produce some ghosts that can haunt us pretty badly. We may think we've done our job well, but unfortunately, most people resent being walked over and can get vindictive in a hurry. And when they hit back, it's usually with a much harder blow than we gave them in the first place.

Ignoring the others sometimes is very tempting. "If they don't want to cooperate, just let them go their way, I'll go mine." It seems so simple, but it rarely works. All it takes is for the boss to say, "Did you check this out with George?" or "Will this fit into the time slot with Helen's project?" Now we've got problems. We've either got to admit that we failed to check it out, or try to alibi (a lie by I), or go back and take the chance of having to do much of our job over, and this time *having* to work with those whom we've deliberately ignored.

All of this matter of cooperating sounds fine, but it really isn't that easy. There are some built-in traps, for instance. We want our people to be loyal. We want them to respect us as their leader. We would like to hear them say that they work for the best group in the organization. That's great—or is it? Loyalty is fine, but it can also work against us. People often find it easier to be loyal to a small group than to a large organization, so they develop strong feelings about the work group, even refusing promotions to other groups, or being disgruntled when they are moved somewhere for the betterment of the organization. This means their loyalty really isn't to the organization, but to a supervisor or a group of fellow workers. This isn't necessarily bad; it just becomes bad when it causes the organization's overall goals to suffer. When our people begin to compete with other groups to the extent that there are hard feelings, or one group takes advantage of another, then it is bad.

Another problem is that resentment builds among supervisors, which is often the beginning of jealousy. We don't like to admit that we are jealous, but let the boss spend too much time with some of our coordinates, and we begin to wonder if the boss likes them or their work better than ours. Again we see the immaturity coming out. Lack of confidence will produce the same results. We may feel that we can't really compete on the performance level, so we start to look for other things to make up the difference in our relationship with the boss. We may start a whisper campaign against a fellow supervisor; we may resort to infighting; we may even find ways of telling the boss that the other supervisors have some weaknesses. We may tell the boss about foul-ups that he or she might have missed if we hadn't brought them up. Of course, the boss shouldn't think better of us for doing such a thing, but even if he or she does, we have probably weakened our position in the organization. One of these days we are going to find ourselves needing some help from someone we have reported to the boss, or hoping that the boss doesn't find out about a mess we've made and may be desperately trying to get straightened out. At that time, we may look longingly for a friend and not find one!

## MAKE IT WORK

How do we get the job done? How do we get the cooperation that it takes to get along and get the work out at the same time? Perhaps the one word that comes the closest to being the key is *communication*. The old saying, "We're usually down on what we're not up on" is just as true here as anywhere else. We need to know what's going on in the other groups and it's worth our time to find out. We'll appreciate our fellow-workers' jobs a lot more if we know something about their problems and the reasons for what they're doing. And the same is true about their appreciating what we're trying to do—they need to know where we're trying to go, how we plan to get there, and who we have working to get us there.

We need to anticipate possible conflicts and problems before they have gone too far to be stopped. We need to get into the habit of giving out as much information as possible to those we work with. We should learn to *communicate*. When we find ourselves saying to someone, "But

I told you . . ." we're actually admitting that we don't know very much about communicating. Telling rarely is communicating. One good practice is to get into the habit of writing memos and notes to the people we work with, letting them know what projects we are working on that might need their help, or that might either complement theirs or conflict in some way. The obvious fact is that they will be in a better position to help us if they know what we're doing. Equally important, if they know something of what we're doing, they will be better able to answer questions that arise from their subordinates about our work.

Another simple habit to get into is checking with our coordinates when there is something we don't understand about their job. If one of their employees gets crossways with one of ours, don't just go and jump on somebody. Go calmly and get some facts. We aren't obligated to start a fight whenever one of our people has a problem with someone outside the group. That's building the wrong kind of loyalty. Our people may think we're great for doing it, but we aren't really helping them, ourselves, or the situation by storming around from office to office telling people off. And remember, we shouldn't even pretend that we're "going to get this straightened out once and for all," implying that we will jump on somebody about this. That, too, builds the wrong kind of loyalty. In the long run, our people will respect us more if we provide a smooth working environment for them, and fairly harmonious relations with the others with whom they must associate.

## AVOID LEARNING THE WRONG THING

One more problem we have to deal with as new supervisors is what we do around those people who have been in the organization for a long time and for one reason or another have grown bitter. There is a sort of "bitterness syndrome" that affects some people. They don't like certain policies that affect them; they don't like the way promotions are handled; they don't like the way their raises have been coming or the amount; they feel they should be higher in the organization or should be consulted more or should be making more money. Perhaps even worse, they may see us as a threat to their own security. They may feel that the new people have a better chance than they do, so will resent us and make life a little hard for us. Most of us can handle that, because we see through it easily enough. It's the same problem we faced in school when we made better grades than a classmate who had been considered the better student for a long time. It's like the time we outran a person in a race, when they were faster or older than we were, but for some reason on this occasion we just outran them. The people who will give us the most trouble are those who do know their jobs, who are respected for their knowledge, and one of them may even be the person we've been assigned to, to learn some of the ropes. When this person has a tainted streak or is bitter, it affects us a lot more.

What can we do about such a situation? The best thing to start off doing is to *ignore it.* Certainly we shouldn't try to correct the person nor try any mindchanging. To start off with, we're going to lose the argument just on the basis of experience and knowledge alone. These people will know more arguments and more ways to offset ours than we'll ever be able to handle. So we just leave that idea alone. We could try to present another side of the picture as we see it or as we've been treated, but this has the same problem. In showing us where we've misinterpreted the data, they may even "convert" us to their way of thinking. In the beginning, the best thing for us to do is simply listen and *not respond.*

Later, as we get more confidence or more facts, we might try to deal with the people who are like this—but at first, let them alone. There is always the possibility that they're right, but in the beginning we really can't tell, so saying nothing will serve us longer than anything else we do. Sooner or later we've got to stand on our own feet. We've got to come to our own conclusions about the organization, about the boss, about our particular work group, and about the specific job we're working on. The sooner we do it, the better, but we ought to make sure that it's our own thinking we're doing, not that of the older and "wiser" heads around us. Just as they have more information, they also have more biases. At least we ought to wait until we've developed our own biases before we become bitter or start to disapprove of the way the organization is run.

Another thing we're going to have to do someday is develop our own standard of behavior. We may not realize it, but at first we really don't have a standard. We act like the people around us; we ask them how we should feel about things, how we should act and even what kind of action is preferable. At some point in time we need to ask ourselves, "Is this really me, or am I still just parroting what I've heard?" We need to decide for ourselves how we feel about the boss, the organization, etc., and it ought to be based on as much fact and experience as possible. Above all, *it ought to be us.*

## CONCLUSION

Our ability to get along with the people we work with is one test of our maturity. After all, we're all working for the same organization with the same long-range goals. The advantages of having a peaceful environment to work in are obvious. We need to be careful in building loyalties, to see that they are built around the organization as a whole, not just to us or our small group. When we work with others under the same boss, we need to realize that in the long run, cooperation is the key to getting the job done satisfactorily. Cutting throats or ignoring others in our work and planning may seem the quickest way, but it lacks a lot of being the surest way. The best way is to learn to communicate—not by telling, but by being sure that the fellow-workers get a memo or a note from us letting them in on what we're doing and suggesting ways in which getting together might help both of us. These aren't the only times we need to communicate with them, of course. We need to talk to them about possible conflicts or problems that arise among our subordinates. But the getting together should be pleasant, not an effort to build our prestige among our own people. They may think we're great, but that probably won't help the organization in the long run. The thing that's the most likely to help is for us to develop a good working relationship with our coordinates so that the situation will be conducive to productive work.

## EXERCISES

1. Group discussion: In almost any organization, there is competition among the various groups working for the same department head or even for the same boss. There must be some reasons why this happens. Come up with a list of why it happens in an organization, and why it seems to be common in any type of work area. Record this list for discussion in the next two exercises.

2. Group discussion: Using the group's findings from above, come up with a group consensus as to whether the effect of this competitiveness is good or bad. In other words, if it did not exist, would the organization be better off or worse off?

3. Individual assignment: Let each person look at the list, and think of ways he or she could avoid having each one of the items happen in his or her sphere of influence. This is a long assignment, and each person should consider each item. When all have, the group

should discuss each item to find the simplest way to avoid the competition, in those cases where the members feel the competition should be eliminated.

4. Subgroup activity: In small groups, come up with a policy statement that could be put into effect in the organization that would deal with the problem of poor communication. This ought to be explicit enough to describe what any supervisor should do, and what he or she should tell the subordinates. (This is a *team-building* exercise, and very important. Each person should think in terms of *what* he or she would like to know, *when* they should know it, and how often there should be a *review process* for looking at the communications. The statement should also deal with the accountability for the communications effort, that is, who should be responsible for seeing that the communications effort is made, and what the consequences are for failure to do it.)

# 5
# THE IMPORTANCE OF
# GOOD COMMUNICATIONS

## COMMUNICATING—GOOD OR BAD?

It's easy to tell people they should be good communicators; it's much harder to tell them *how* to be good communicators. One problem is that we aren't always sure just what we mean by "good communications." The preacher who presents a great sermon gets rousing support (orally) from the congregation, but when someone asks what the sermon was about, very few may be able to answer correctly. When the politician holds an audience spellbound, and then they go out and vote for someone else, he or she may have failed to communicate. As supervisors, we are most often transmitting messages that should produce some action, change something, or speak to the action that has already been carried out—if only to say that it was right or wrong. What is good communicating in this kind of situation?

We might define good communicating as getting the right message to the right source in an efficient manner. Notice that we said "in an *efficient* manner," not necessarily the cheapest, nor the quickest, nor the easiest. Efficient means *correct,* also. The reason for saying it this way is that so often we take the easy way out and just *tell* somebody something. But since memory is not very reliable, this isn't a very efficient method. Pretty soon we will find that the person we told will have to be told again, or that he or she is doing it wrong, or has somehow got the message all fouled up. Perhaps another word we could use is *effective.* Effective carries yet another implication—that the message got through and the correct results have come from the action taken. When we send a message, we should think to ourselves, "It isn't enough to be sure that it *can* be understood; I must be sure that it will be very difficult to *misunderstand* it."

## FOUR ELEMENTS IN COMMUNICATING

We can understand communicating better if we tear it down and look at the parts or elements that go to make up any communication effort.

In essence, there are four basic elements that we can look at, namely the *sender,* the *receiver,* the *message,* and the *environment* or conditions under which the message is sent. Each of these things affects the results, and the effectiveness of our communication depends on how well we take each one into consideration. For example, the most powerful speaker you know will have trouble when the room is hot, or when the audience is uncomfortable in some way. This doesn't mean that that speaker can't do a better job than someone else; it means that he or she could be even more effective under better circumstances. On the other hand, when the person we're talking to really wants the information we're presenting, and is eager to hang on to every word, our presentation can be pretty poor and still get across. *But it could get across better if we were doing a better job.* When I'm bragging to the car pool about my success at fishing, I doubt seriously that I'm getting through very much, especially if traffic happens to be bad; but when I'm talking to a mother whose son I've just seen in a distant city, I expect the message will get across much better. Finally, when my son wants me to pick him up from someplace so he won't have to walk home, he goes into much detail and even repeats what he's said so there will be no misunderstanding.

Note that there is a difference in emphasis on where the breakdown is in effective communication. A different element is involved in each case. In the fishing story, neither the subject matter nor the environment was conducive to successful transmission. In talking to the mother about her son, the message was very important to her, and the receiver (mother) was ready to hang on to every word. When my son talks to me about giving him a ride, I may not be very interested in the message, but to him it is all important. And it is important to him as the sender to see that I (as the receiver) get the message. There are several things to notice here about effective communication. First there is the fact that different conditions exist when we transmit information. Next there is the fact that the sender and the receiver have different degrees of interest in the subject matter. The simple truth is that it is rare for the sender to have the same feeling toward the message that the receiver has. But if we fail to take this into consideration when we try to communicate to someone, we may lose the message.

One problem we have is that as senders we always want to put the responsibility for successful communication on the receiver rather than to accept it ourselves. We always react the same way when someone fails to get what we were saying. We think (or say), "But I *told* him . . ."

The first thing we tend to do is to rationalize that if the receiver had listened, he or she would have gotten the message. And that's what it is, *rationalization*. We are failing to accept the responsibility for taking all the elements into consideration. Did we realize that the receiver wasn't getting the message? Did we realize that he or she may not have been interested, and we should have done something to stir up that interest? Did we consider that the environment might not have been the best for good communicating? Were the doors open and others listening in? Was the phone ringing? Was the receiver waiting to see the boss? Were there other distractions either in the office or in his or her mind? Was the receiver really just tolerating our conversation, waiting for the chance to begin his or her own monologue? Did we choose the right time and the right place to discuss the subject? Did we prepare the receiver for the discussion by making it clear what it was we were going to discuss?

These are all important considerations, each one of which can help or hurt the effectiveness of our communications. We can't choose to pay attention to them or ignore them; if we ignore them, they will still tend to disrupt our communicating efforts. What usually happens is that we use about the same approach each time, except in very critical situations. We say things the same way to different people, regardless of the circumstances or whether the person we're talking to is interested. We wouldn't dare approach the boss for a raise and promotion

in the same manner we would ask for a sandwich in a restaurant, but what about the times between those extremes when we probably should take a little more care in the way we choose our words and our approach? Unfortunately, the *natural* approach is to put things in *our own* frame of reference, on the basis of our interest, our vocabulary, our need for telling. What we *should* do, of course, is to put all of our conversation and other types of communication in the *receiver's* frame of reference, but this is a lot easier said than done. *We just don't think that way.*

## THE RECEIVER HAS A DIFFERENT FREQUENCY

We think in terms of *our* goals, *our* interests, *our* needs, *our* problems—not the *receiver's* goals, interests, needs, problems. When we communicate, we do it successfully by either tuning in on the receiver's frequency or getting the receiver to tune in on ours. The chances are pretty good that both the sender and the receiver desire that the other make the change. But the sender generally has the message that needs to be transmitted, and so should accept the responsibility of seeing that both are on the same frequency.

Perhaps one of the best things we can do before we try communicating is ask ourselves what frequency the receiver is on. In other words: "What is there about this message that would make Fred think he wants to get it? It's important to me, why should it be important to him? I know he needs it, but does *he* know it?" When we've decided what the receiver's frequency is, then we must decide whether, if we were the receiver, we would get the message from the communication we're preparing. To put it another way, we must ask: "Is this the best way to get the message across to Ruth? Will she really read this memo or this bulletin? Will she read it carefully enough to see that it was meant for her or that it is a completely new policy, different from the one she is familiar with?" There are plenty of cases on record in which important new policy changes have been put into letters and lost completely by the time they have gotten down to the people who were supposed to use them.

## BARRIERS TO EFFECTIVE COMMUNICATING

This brings us to the important point of looking at some of the barriers to good communicating. Take the case of losing a new policy by putting it into a letter and sending it down through the organization. To an outsider, reading the letter for the first time, it may appear that this is perfectly clear and that there is no reason for a breakdown. A closer examination, however, may show that many letters go up and down through the organization every day, carrying insignificant details. Those who receive them have learned through experience that rarely does anything important come to them this way, and when it does, there will also be a big announcement made by someone else at the same time. This means to them, "If it's really important, somebody will tell us without us spending a lot of time reading useless material." (This ought to also be a lesson for first-line supervisors: Be alert enough to catch important messages without having to be told by some other source.) We'll list the first barrier, then, as hiding important messages among those that the receiver has learned aren't very significant.

The second barrier is the other side of the coin—sending unimportant messages. It just doesn't make good business sense to send messages about which we can think, "Oh well, nobody ever reads these things anyway." It doesn't take us long to get into some sloppy habits writing with this thought in mind. Equally senseless is the idea of writing just to move the responsibility to someone else's shoulders: "I did my part; I wrote a letter covering it." This, in fact, becomes an unnecessary message, or perhaps even a much more damaging communication than none at all. This is a third barrier, if we consider that our motives weren't very honest in the first place. We aren't likely to work very hard at making a message clear if we have ulterior motives in sending it. After all, what we're really trying to do in such a case is hide the truth, so what better way to do it than in garbled communication.

And even when we have the best of intentions we run into another barrier: overkill. It's so important and so vital that everyone get the message that we go into too much detail or give too many facts. As a result, the real message gets smothered by a lot of background information that belongs right there—in the background. The problem comes when we start to *sell* the idea instead of just giving out the necessary information. When we start selling, we almost always go too far, often raising questions in the receivers' minds about things that aren't really important to the subject we are discussing. Contrary to what may seem logical, it is usually better to give too little information than too much. Too much not only raises questions, but may get the receivers to thinking about something that they are particularly opposed to, or about which they have already made some kind of judgment. When they get to thinking about that, the real message is bound to suffer, and probably get lost. Trying to get it across the second time is going to be much harder than the first, too.

This suggests yet another barrier to good communication, the matter of organizing the message. If we hide the message among unnecessary information, it can't help but get lost. By the same token, if we organize it so poorly that the receiver gets confused trying to find out what we're really trying to say, we might as well not have sent the message in the first place. Let's do a little thinking about how to organize: It stands to reason that the more time we spend leading up to an important point, the easier it will be for the receiver to get lost or lose interest. So one of the ways we can organize profitably is to get the important part of the message out as quickly as possible. Start off by saying what it is we are trying to get across. "This is to recommend that we proceed with the project outlined below," or, "Starting tomorrow the salary structure is being changed." If nothing else happens, at least we will get the person's attention! Those who know about such things tell us that we remember longest the first and last things we hear or read. This means that the closing shot at the receiver should also contain either a summary or a conclusion. In another chapter we'll deal specifically with writing; for now let's notice one of the ways this barrier works against most letter writers. When we write a letter we say what we want to say, offer answers to problems, give out the necessary information—then don't know how to close the letter. Instead of just stopping, we look for some way to end it. Almost without exception, we use some kind of trite phrase that is impersonal and stuffy sounding. "If we can be of any further assistance to you in this or any other matter, please do not hesitate to call on us." If it's true that we remember the first and last thing we read, then what will the reader remember about us? Not that we are willing to help, but that we are very unfriendly and use form letters to send our messages! If there's nothing at all friendly and helpful by the time we get to the end of the letter, the reader isn't likely to believe it just because we use some worn out phrase.

One more barrier we want to talk about is the matter of trying to communicate with people that have different slants or different kinds of information. This difference in viewpoint will cause the message to be lost or confused before it does its job for us. For example, when we talk to the nonsupervisory people who work for us about something the company wants, we have to remember that their views of the company are quite different from ours. Even their loyalties are different from ours. So we have to realize that they will likely receive the message as meaning something else if we put it in terms of "the company." Of course, education, experience, and other background factors play a big part in our ability to communicate and are a part of this same barrier. The employee who is struggling to make ends meet or is worried about the next house payment while adding a new bathroom for the relative who has just come to live with them isn't likely to get the message that says that the company's new long-range savings plan is a good investment even if it means "doing without" for the time being.

## APPLICATION

Now let's go back and look at some of these barriers and see how they work in real life. Take the matter of hiding the important messages among the less important ones. Let's consider the supervisor who has a large number of people working for him or her and sometimes finds it necessary to get important messages to them—but is unable to call large group meetings because of the nature of the job. A particularly important policy change has come up and it is necessary to get it to the people as soon as possible. The choices are: (a) call the people in smaller groups until all of them have been covered, (b) pass around a memorandum to all of them, (c) appoint several to come in and get the message and then take it to the rest of the people, or (d) post the message on the bulletin board. Which is the wisest choice?

First, let's make sure that we understand that in supervision there is often no clear-cut right or wrong. There are advantages and disadvantages, and the decision really depends on which has the fewest drawbacks. So how do we get the new policy matter to the employees? Let's see what is likely to happen if we choose (d), putting the message on the bulletin board. If the board is like many, there will be all kinds of insignificant things there, from lost dogs to cars for sale. But even if it is reasonably clean, the bulletin board offers several drawbacks. It gives us no assurance that all of the employees will see the notice unless we contact them individually and remind them to look at it. But while we were telling them this, we could also have given them the policy message in the first place.

How about (b), having a memorandum passed around to all of the employees? This has the advantage of seeing that everyone gets the message at the same time and in the same words. But if there are likely to be questions, this isn't very good, because the people they will ask are others like themselves who got their information from the same memorandum. Maybe the best thing to do is to choose (c): call a group in and brief them, then have them take the message back to the rest of the employees. There are some real advantages to this idea, even though it sounds as though it would take the same amount of time as calling in all the people in small groups, since that's what we will be expecting the group leaders to do. The advantage of (c) is that we will have a chance to sell the leaders; then they will be doing the selling of the new policy to the rest of the employees. In the long run, this may work out best. But here again there is the danger of having the employees get the wrong story, since it will be coming from several people instead of one. This can be corrected by having the memorandum discussed earlier sent out with a note that there will be group meetings later in which they can ask questions. If we do a good job of briefing the leaders, our work is reduced considerably. The final choice is (a), do all the briefing ourselves. If we think there will be any problems about the work group accepting the policy change from one of their own members, then we shouldn't hesitate to call the small group meetings and get the policy across as best we can.

Let's look at the idea of "overkilling" the message. We have decided that a certain idea suggested by one of our employees is a great one and we want to pass it on up the line to higher management. In an effort to

prove what a good idea this is we decide it would be well to give some background information on both the employee who came up with the idea, and the need for the idea itself. We want to do a fair job of presenting both the employee and the idea, so we really lay it on pretty thick. Of course the results are obvious—we oversell, and by the time the people who might be interested get through wading through all of the nonessentials, they have lost interest, and we have lost a chance to sell a good idea and do a favor for a deserving employee.

## HOW CAN WE IMPROVE COMMUNICATION?

So far we have talked about the barriers and other things that might hinder us from getting the message across. What are some things we can do to really get the job of communicating done effectively? First and foremost, we must get the message straight ourselves! After all, it was only an idea in our mind when it all started. It wasn't full-grown, nor was it in any shape to be transmitted to someone else. But if we go right on ahead and start to explain it without first getting the whole picture straight in our own thinking, we're in for trouble. The next thing we can do is to try and *sell* the idea. The fact that we think it is a great idea or plan doesn't necessarily mean everyone else will, especially since they probably have a few ideas of their own. Just trying to force our ideas down someone's throat isn't likely to get us very far. Another thing to do is to get the message out in the open. We sometimes try to sneak an unpleasant idea or change by someone by hiding it between two pleasant things. The end result may be that we were successful—at least successful in hiding the idea. There's nothing better than tact when it comes to handling unpleasant messages—we should use it and whatever other human relations tools we can—but in the end we must make sure the real message stands out and gets recognized. If we want to correct tardiness, sloppy work, poor writing, bad attitudes, or anything else, we'd better be sure that the employees know these are the things we are talking about. The situation may even be unpleasant, but at least the message won't get lost!

Next, we should make certain the message gets there. It's not enough that we know what we plan to say, nor that we say it. It's only successful communication *when the message gets to the receivers.* How will we know that? Not just because we can say, "Don't you remember, I told you . . ." We will only know for sure when we hear them tell us what's been said. We want to know how they hear the message, what it meant to them, how they have interpreted our remarks. Successful communicators have different ways of getting this feedback. Some will simply ask the person they're talking to what that person has heard. This tends to put the responsibility on the hearer, but is effective. Others may ask the person to give them some feedback because they aren't sure they're communicating the message as well as they ought to. This keeps some of the blame for the misunderstanding (if there is any) on the communicator. Still others try to get their feedback in the form of results from the message sent. They'll ask the hearers what action is planned as a result of the message they've heard. As the sender hears certain action plans, he or she will now know just what the hearers heard and how it was understood. Whatever way we get it, we must be sure that we don't rely just on our own confidence in ourselves as communicators. We may be good, but we can be better and we aren't as good at one time as we are at another. Also, we are not as good with certain people and with certain messages as we are with others.

The third part of good communicating is the *ability to listen.* Listening is a skill; it must be learned and it can be forgotten even after we've learned it! Of all the skills of communicating, listening is the hardest to learn and the hardest to practice with any kind of consistency. As a matter of fact, the more we communicate, the more we are likely to forget to use this skill. We get so used to hearing our own voice and so used to saying things in ways that sound good *to us,* that we forget that everyone isn't always tuned into our voice or our message. Listening is more than just being quiet. It means that we listen for content. We listen for meanings. We listen to see if our message has gotten through. We try not to get into the habit of hearing what we want to hear instead of what is really being said. When we are doing a good job of listening, we don't interrupt people, nor do we jump right in at the end of their sentence with a quick response because we can't stand silence. We pause, if necessary, until we've processed the information we've just received. We repeat the statements or facts if we've got any doubt about whether we heard right. We even ask for clarification if there's any chance of our misunderstanding something. Of course, we don't do this all the time. But we don't hesitate to do it if there's room for doubt. We learn to effectively use such phrases as, "Do I hear you saying . . ." and "Let me see if I have this straight . . ." and "The points you are making, as I hear them, are . . ." Again, we don't use these expressions all the time, but we aren't afraid of admitting that we may not be getting all that's sent.

Finally, we can summarize these skills in this way. They've been classified as the skills of good communicators:

1. Knowing the message
2. Knowing that the message got there
3. Listening

Remember, these are skills. They have to be learned, and as we move up in the organization we tend to fall back on the first one: *Know the message.* We see ourselves as well informed. We've communicated a lot in our lives, so we naturally consider ourselves pretty good at it. So we stop listening, and that means we've lost any chance for good feedback. In the absence of feedback, we have only our own knowledge of the subject to fall back on, and we may not be as good as we think we are. The key: *We can always be better at communicating.*

## CONCLUSION

Much has been said about communicating. In fact, it's the "much saying" that has made communicating so hard to do. There's a lot more talking going on than there is listening, and there's a lot more talking going on than is being understood. To make things worse, most people who are poor communicators don't know it and even blame others for not understanding what is said. Because there are always at least two people involved in any communicating effort, there is the problem that each can blame the other, with neither accepting that blame. The solution to good communicating is neither simple nor something that can be done overnight. There are skills involved and these skills are often difficult to learn. The best solution is for the supervisor to develop some ways of checking how he or she communicates, so that at least one party in the communicating effort will be aware of the problem. The steps that were offered are offered again: Know the message, know that the message got there, and listen. The listening is the most difficult part to learn, but it is the most valuable part of the three. It is through the listening that we get the feedback for knowing whether the message got there. If we aren't very good at getting the message there initially, the knowledge that it didn't make it at least gives us a chance to try again. Somewhere down the line we'll begin to get good at getting the message there!

## EXERCISES

1. Group activity: Have one person write down the following information: when and where he or she was born, when he or she came to work with the organization, when he or she made supervisor, and the name of one person working for him or her. Then have the writer *whisper* that information to another person, who whispers it to a third, and so on until the message gets around the room. Have the last person to receive it write it down. The first should then read the information that was started, and the last reads the information he or she received.

2. Individual activity: The activity above is one that is often used at parties to show how messages get messed up, but in this case we're serious about finding out how to communicate more effectively. To get this information, the following activities should be undertaken: Individually, each person should write down what his or her *feelings* were before, during, and after the exercise above. Next, there should be small-group discussions of the same thing. The findings should be presented and recorded for the whole group to discuss.

3. Group discussion: Have the whole group decide whether any of the feelings listed in exercise 2 exist in our communications efforts within the organization. Look for such things as: "I wasn't

interested." "I didn't care." "I thought it wasn't very important." "I couldn't remember." Have the group discuss these things and decide whether they make our communications poor within the real world where we work.

4. Subgroup activity (a workshop): In every organization there are communications problems, most of which could be eliminated or at least improved. Have each subgroup look at the real world in which each of its members works, and decide what are the most serious communications problems within each person's part of the organization. Spell out the problem in enough detail so that it can be dealt with. Be sure not to offer the solution, just the problem. (Of course, sometimes the problem offers the solution. For example, "The boss doesn't tell me anything," suggests that the solution is to have the boss tell more. It doesn't really spell out the exact problem, though. Why doesn't the boss tell me more? And how much more; what kinds of things; when should I be told? All of these need to be dealt with.) The solutions will come in the next exercise. *Note:* When problems are finally defined to the satisfaction of the subgroup, they should be put in priority order. Which of these problems are the most critical? Which should be dealt with first? Which would have the greatest payoff? And so on. Taking all of these things into consideration, rank the findings in order of importance.

5. Group exercise: Combine the problems from the subgroups and see if there is any similarity among the top-ranked items of communications problems. Look at those at (or near) the top of most lists and decide how best to tackle them. Before ending this discussion, a decision should be made to take some kind of action or to recommend to the organization what action to take. Take only one problem at a time during the consideration, and don't try to solve them all. At a later time others can be considered.

# 6
# SETTING UP THE WORK (PLANNING AND ORGANIZING)

As we have already seen, our job as supervisors is to get work done through other people. We are doing our best work when we deal with the problems of getting the job accomplished, rather than doing the work ourselves. While we have the direct responsibility for the workers and how they do, we still are not supposed to do the work ourselves. (Of course, emergencies arise, but we're talking about the normal activities of a supervisor.)

## SUPERVISORS AS MANAGERS

Some people make a distinction between "supervisor" and "manager." For our purposes in this and the next chapter we will talk about the supervisor's job of *managing*. Since the usual definition of a manager is "one who gets the job done through people," we won't do any harm if we use the terms interchangeably. Any supervisor has certain managing responsibilities. We will want to see what that means to us, the new supervisors.

Everyone above the worker or specialist level has some managing to do. The only difference between the first-line supervisor and the head of the organization is the scope and responsibility of their managing assignments. Basically, every manager, whether the top executive or a foreman, has four managing functions to perform:

Planning

Organizing

Directing

Controlling

The first two we'll discuss in this chapter, the last two in the next. While all supervisors have all of these functions, the extent to which they do each of them usually depends on their level in the organization. For instance, top executives would probably spend most of their time planning and organizing, while first-line supervisors should devote most of their time to directing and controlling the activities of people. Now, since all supervisors have all of these functions, let's see what they *really* mean to the new supervisor.

## PLANNING

First, let's be sure we understand something about *all* of these functions. Each is something that is done along with, and as a part of, the job. While we should learn each as a skill and be aware of the fact that we are doing it, we shouldn't be scared off because it has a fancy name. The chances are pretty good we'll do some of each one whether on purpose or by accident. So when we talk about planning, we're talking about the everyday job—how it's done, what will be done tomorrow, where we hope to go from there.

Planning is by far the most important of all the activities we've listed because everything else results from it. It is simply the means by which supervisors decide in what direction they want their group to go. The process can be carefully done or it can be haphazard. The interesting thing is that even *doing nothing* will still produce a result! The organization will still exist, tomorrow will still come, and the employees will do something, right or wrong. Most experts agree that planning is the most important of all the functions, and this is one reason why: the organization will not stop just because we fail to plan. It may well get off the track or head in the wrong direction, but it will still struggle along.

Another reason for the importance of planning is that it's much harder to correct the results of poor planning than to do it correctly in the first place. The results of poor planning can be pretty disastrous, and, unfortunately for the new supervisor, they usually show up more quickly for him than for the higher management. When top management makes a mistake in planning, it sometimes takes many months or even years for it to come to light. When the first-line supervisor makes poor plans it sometimes is only a matter of *hours* before the results are known. If an executive decides to spend more money on advertising to boost the sale of a certain product, it may take a year to see whether the campaign was a success. If a supervisor plans his or her work force incorrectly, and has too many people off during a peak period, the resulting slowdown in production will be known before the day is over.

### How and what to plan

How do we as supervisors plan our work? Obviously we want to consider whatever alternatives are available to us and select the best one, all things considered. Too often supervisors think of planning as deciding to do—or not to do—*one certain thing.* Good planning always takes into consideration all the possible alternatives, weighs them carefully, then selects the one with the most merit. There is a caution here, though: *Don't* try to find the perfect solution, or the one that has no drawbacks. *There seldom is such a plan.* In fact, we may have to settle for the plan with the fewest drawbacks, because none of the plans is completely satisfactory.

We form our plans by making four basic decisions:

1. What is to be done?
2. Who is to do it?
3. How is it to be done?
4. When is it to be done?

Now let's take these one at a time and see how they fit into the day-to-day job.

**1. What is to be done?**   We should have this definitely in mind before we go on to any of the other questions. For example, it isn't enough to decide that we are going to give the people some more training, then go out and find someone to do the training. We must first decide exactly what training is needed, how much we can do ourselves, how much can be done by someone else, and how much can just be left undone. If we aren't careful, we'll find ourselves trying to carry out plans that weren't very definite to start with; this results in a lot of muddling around trying to make something work that didn't have a very good start. So the rule here is to be sure that we know exactly where it is we're going before we start to go there. It isn't necessary to write all our plans down, but it sometimes helps us understand what we are going to do if we record on a note pad a positive statement of just exactly what we plan. Of course, the plan may change as we go along, but at least we have *something to change.* Otherwise we'll end up making our plans as we go, changing those, repeating our errors, and in general botching it all up.

**2. Who is to do it?**   Part of planning is to determine whether this is a project for the whole work force, for just a few of them, or for one individual. If it is a one-time job, there is a great advantage in having only one or a few people work on the project. It's easier to keep up with a special project if only a few people are involved and less training time will be required. On the other hand, if the work is the kind that will continue to be a part of the responsibility of our work group, then our planning should include deciding how soon we want everyone to learn the new work.

There is an important training note here: If we aren't careful, we may let a job just gradually slip into being. No one is ever really trained for it, but finally everyone is doing it—and probably not very well. We may have it in mind that *one of these days* we'll do the training, but we keep putting it off until a more convenient time—which never comes. A basic fact to remember about training is that like everything else on the job it must be *planned for*. Left alone, it will not happen. The good supervisor plans for it to happen!

**3. How is it to be done?**   Once a goal or objective has been decided (and agreed) on, we still have to decide how it's going to be met. This decision has to be considered at every level, but especially at the first level. *Policies* about the work will be set at higher level. The decisions about the *actual work* are usually made at that point in the organization where the work is to be carried on, hence the first-level supervision. (The decisions may not always be made here because some supervisors *give up* some authority to their bosses. Then they complain because they don't have enough authority to carry out their jobs, when in reality they didn't use it when they had it.)

Policy setting is sometimes done unconsciously, because we can set policy by *doing nothing*. If we don't come up with firm policies on matters such as overtime, safety, time off, promotions, or appraisals, precedents will begin to set the policies for us. If we intend to do a job without adding employees, we may be setting a policy for more overtime toward the end of the job!

**4. When is it to be done?**   The final question to be decided has to do with one of the most important ingredients in successful planning: time. While the obvious conclusion is that the completion date is the most important consideration in time, this is only part of the story. No deadline is missed *all of a sudden*. Long-range plans usually fall through because of poor *short-range* planning. As first-level supervisors, we are seldom directly involved in the long-range objectives of the organization, but we often are very much involved in the short-range plans. So meeting these short-range objectives is the most important "time" aspect of our role in planning.

### Understanding the plan

It's almost too obvious to mention, but no plan is very good if it isn't understood by those affected by it. The reason for mentioning it is that we tend to blame someone else when a plan begins to go awry. The first thing we should investigate is whether or not the planning included safeguards against misunderstanding the plan. Were the employees informed? How were they informed? Were they just told or did they get an opportunity to ask questions, seek additional information and generally get familiar with what was expected of them?

This sounds like something pretty big that would only be done when some major operation is undertaken. Not so. The employees need to know what's expected of them even in a small, one-hour assignment. Remember, our people are more interested in the day-to-day activity than in the long-range operations, so it's the smaller things that are important at this level.

### Who's watching the clock?

Something that should concern us all as supervisors is the fact that since higher management is interested in the "big picture" (i.e., the long-range objectives), they usually aren't watching the short-range objectives nearly as much. This means they may do no more than read an occasional progress report, always keeping an eye toward the final completion date. If we first-line supervisors aren't careful, we may be the only ones watching the short-range dates. We can be sure a lot of people will be looking, though, when it's too late to do anything about it.

Sometimes at first-level we may get the delusion that everybody is watching everything, and that we're just insignificant little cogs in a giant wheel. But once we've been trapped by this thinking, we're heading for trouble, especially with short-range plans. Even though everyone seems to be watching over our shoulder, they still expect us to watch the day-by-day progress of the work. For example, if the long-range objective is to reduce absenteeism, higher management will be concerned with quarterly, or perhaps monthly reports, but we—and the other first-line supervisors—must worry about who shows up and who doesn't *every day*.

## Objectives and policy

Planning, then, is a function of management in which we are concerned with the future of the organization in those operations for which we are responsible. In the process of planning, we decide where we are going and how we intend to get there. Usually, we call "where we are going" the *objective* and "how to get there" the *policy*. Some have compared this to a ship taking a trip. The objective is the destination of the ship, while policy is the course the ship must take to get there. In a sense, planning is the rudder steering the ship. The supervisor doing the planning controls the ship, and without planning the ship has no rudder.

While it won't be dealt with in detail in this chapter, we should learn quickly that the more we take our people into the planning effort, the more likely we are to reach the objective. Since we are more likely to be involved in short-term planning, we are setting short-term objectives, often with short-term policies. These may well be day-to-day type things that our people know as much about as we do. Getting them to assist in setting deadlines is a good way to also get commitment to these deadlines. Getting them to participate in laying the ground rules is a good way to motivate them to work according to these ground rules.

## A brief word about controlling

In the next chapter we'll talk in detail about the function of controlling. We need to mention it here because planning and controlling are very closely associated with each other. The supervisor controls according to the planning that has been done. For example, budgeting is a type of planning, but the budget itself is a control. While it is being prepared, the budget is part of the planning function. Once the operation is begun, it becomes part of the controlling function.

Other examples might be quality control or service standards. Determining the organization's policies on quality or service is a basic part of *planning*. When those policies go into operation, they are actually *controls*. The importance of all of this is that we should be glad that budgets, standards, and controls exist, because it is through them that the desired end result is reached. They not only direct the way and tell us when we've reached the objective, but they give us a standard to measure against all along the way.

## ORGANIZING

So far we've talked about only a part of what is necessary to set up the work. There is another function called *organizing* that plays a big part in getting us to the final objective we have set. Organizing is a pretty broad term and generally includes two things: the *structure* of the organization we have set up to do the job and the *people* in this organization. Since higher management usually handles the structure of organization, we'll look mostly at that part of organizing concerned with people. First, though, let's note that we aren't talking about something big and complicated when we use the word "organization." We're simply talking about any group of people who have joined together to get something done that they couldn't get done by themselves. This fits the *small work group* in one location as well as it does an entire organization of thousands of people across many states or countries. And the same principles apply.

In Chapter 9 we will talk in detail about interviewing prospective employees, so we won't go into that here. However, since part of organizing includes staffing the organization, we should realize that when it comes time to fill a vacancy in our group we will be expected to do an interview. Also, since the prospective employee will be working in our organization, we should look forward to meeting and finding out as much as possible about him or her. Most new supervisors, however, dread this particular phase of the job. A little knowledge of how to conduct the interview—and a little experience—should cause these fears to diminish considerably.

### Right person—right job

The whole object of the staffing phase of organizing is to try to match up the potential of the employee with the requirements of the job. Unfortunately, we often find that through poor staffing we end up making ourselves and our employees miserable. Often we do a poor job of matching an employee's skills and interests with the job, then blame the employee for poor performance. We should really blame ourselves for poor judgment!

Getting the right people to do the right job makes a lot of sense from a lot of standpoints. Obviously, employees who are doing jobs for which they are well suited have fewer frustrations, see that they are useful to the organization, and feel that they have a chance to be recognized. As a result, they are most likely to be motivated to do their best and will be reasonably satisfied employees. From our standpoint as the supervisor, a lot of our problems are solved, because the employees' motivation should reduce absenteeism and turnover and increase productivity. We will then have more time to handle other phases of our job. From the organization's standpoint, it is not only getting value for wages paid—it is also getting a good picture of *us* in the process. When our people perform well, it naturally reflects favorably on us. Note, too, that a mismatch between employee and job can make all of these things come out unfavorably.

There is another phase of organizing which we will deal with in detail in Chapter 10; that is *training*. It isn't enough to try to get employees and their jobs matched as well as possible. We must still make up the difference between the employees' present skills and the job requirements. This can best be done by training. Given enough time and patience, of course, employees will learn on their own. In fact, many do. But this rarely is the most efficient way or the most practical approach from the organization's standpoint. Not only do we need to have the employees know their job, we need to *know* they know how to do their work. Training gives us this knowledge, because we see that they have had an opportunity to learn the skill. If it's good training, we will see them actually demonstrating their proficiency. Then if they do not do their job properly, we look for some cause other than lack of training.

## CONCLUSION

We have often defined the supervisor's job as getting the job done through other people. However, a portion of the supervisor's job includes some functions that are usually classified as "managerial" rather than "supervisory." They have many different names but we'll classify them into four functions: planning, organizing, directing, controlling. Two of these, planning and organizing, have to do with setting the work up, the other two have to do with getting the work done. The world is full of proverbs about having a goal, but the one that says, "If you don't know where you're going, any road will get you there," best describes the problem of planning. Many organizations never get anywhere because they don't really know where they want to go. Supervisors should think always in terms of planning, planning, planning. As simple as this sounds, it isn't easy to do with all the other things that are going on around the work area and across the desk. Once we've decided what to do, it's equally important to see that the right people are doing it. This comes under the function of organizing. It's not enough just to plan: we must act on that plan. In simple terms, it's a matter of the right people doing the right thing at the right time. Any time the supervisor has control over this function, it's important that attention be paid to it, rather than just let things be done as they always have. When we do it this way and neglect our responsibility, we give rise to the old saying, "There's no special *reason* for doing it this way; we've just *always* done it this way!"

## EXERCISES

1. Group discussion: Generate a list of things that the organization has to plan at least five years ahead. How many of these do we directly contribute to with specific inputs of some kind that help in the decision making? Should we and could we contribute more than we do? Record the list for further discussion.

2. Group discussion: Generate a list of things the organization cannot plan more than a month in advance. How many of these things do we contribute to with specific inputs of some kind that help in the decision making? Should we and could we contribute more than we do? Record this list for further discussion.

3. Half-group discussion: Let half of the group take the list on long-range planning and the other half the short-range planning list. In small subgroups within these halves, decide what information is needed for each of the things planned. Go into as much detail as possible, even down to listing forms or reports that are considered, if applicable. When the subgroups are through, let each half compile their findings.

4. Group discussion: With the lists from exercise 3, see how much the long-range planning is dependent on the short-range results. Compare the two lists to do this. Also, see if there is a similarity or

overlapping in the lists. (This exercise will do much to show the relationship between short- and long-range planning.)

5. Individual activity: Each person should look at his or her own organization and decide how it would be best organized if it did not exist and it was just now being created. The idea is to decide how many people would be required, what their qualifications would be, who would report to whom, etc. In other words, simply make up an organization to do what is now being done.

6. Group activity: Take one of the organizations worked on in exercise 5 above and let the whole group decide how it would be organized if it were done from scratch. This means selecting one the whole group is familiar with, or maybe creating an organization to do one of the tasks the organization now does. Note that one of the requirements is to find out what the goals, plans, and services for that operation are. (It shouldn't be an *expansion* of the work. The end product or service ought to be the same as it is now—or less—so that the group can see that if we were starting over, we'd probably do things differently. As it is, we've used tradition and custom and the existing people to get to the goals we're looking for.)

# 7

# GETTING THE WORK DONE
# (DIRECTING AND CONTROLLING)

All supervisors, no matter how many or how few the people they supervise, can view their job as that of getting the work done through other people. Planning and organizing—discussed in Chapter 6—set the stage for the next two functions, *directing* and *controlling*. The best of plans and the best organization won't do the work. Only those under us can do it, and we must direct them in doing it, and control the efforts they put forth *while* doing it. In most cases, planning and organizing are done at higher levels in the organization, while directing and controlling are done at the lower levels—usually at first levels. So, as new supervisors we must be doubly conscious of the functions of directing and controlling.

## DIRECTING

Of all the functions the supervisors perform, by far the hardest is directing. Directing involves people, and people are complex, often differing from one another, and even changing themselves from one day to the next. People's needs vary as do their ambitions, and as these things change, so does the way they react in given situations. This means that just about the time we have figured out how certain people will react to certain things, they change on us because of something we may not even know about (at home, at church, at the Little League field, etc.) and now react completely differently the next time we say or do something to them.

But the situation isn't hopeless. There are some common grounds on which people react pretty much the same way all the time, and even different people react the same way to certain things. This means that there are some things we can do that will give us a predictable result, even though we do them to people who are otherwise quite different from one another. Once we have found out these things we can build

our "management philosophy" around them. Let's look at some of these things and see if we can't find a basis on which to act and react with our people.

### Facets of directing

There are three facets of directing: leading, communicating, and motivating. Each is a skill, but each is hard to learn and even harder to define.

**Leading**  Let's discuss leadership first. What is leadership? Ask a dozen people and you'll probably get a dozen different answers. It is a vague quality, but one that is recognizable in the people who have it. (More accurately, we can recognize the results of its presence, if not the quality itself.) Perhaps the easiest way to define it is to say that it is "the ability of a supervisor to inspire the workers under him or her to work hard to achieve the goals of the organization." As we see, this is easy to measure, but hard to recognize as a specific thing that a supervisor does to get results.

One thing we know: The idea that leaders are born, not made, is out of date. All of us can be better supervisors than we are. There are things we can learn that will produce better results. There are skills of leadership that can be practiced, learned, and measured. There are, in fact, some characteristics that are shared by people who have been rated as good leaders, and we can develop these as we get more experience and training.

For example, successful leaders usually have the ability to see other people's points of view. They don't necessarily agree with them or give in to them but they at least have some *empathy* for those positions. They are sensitive to other people's problems, and know why people feel the way they do. Successful leaders know how what they say will be taken—how it will affect other individuals. They probably know how those individuals will react to certain things that are done, and when the reaction is different from what they expect, they may even be able to analyze why it's different. Perhaps most important: Successful leaders don't just write off every undesirable behavior to "bad attitude."

Another characteristic good leaders have is the ability to see themselves as others see them. We generally speak of this as self-awareness. Here, again, is the ability to see how what we do will influence others. We should know how what we say will sound from the point of view of others. Will they resent it, miss the point altogether, or agree with it in principle? Good leaders can predict the answer pretty closely. Good leaders will even know their own weaknesses and faults and try to build around them. They don't let such flaws interfere either with their own performance or that of others under them. The important thing about seeing ourselves as others see us is that we are more likely to treat others fairly if we know they are reacting to something we have done or said, and especially if we know why they are reacting that way.

Another characteristic of successful leaders that we can all learn is the willingness to work. There are very few substitutes for hard work, and for leaders there is none. But the kind of hard work leaders do is different from that done by those who are not leaders. Leaders are willing to put in long hours on tasks that are not exciting or rewarding—that may be unpleasant—*just to get the job done.* This doesn't mean that they don't know how to delegate; it means that they don't shirk from those tasks that have to be done sooner or later. When they see that a particular task has to be done, and that it's their job to do it, they tackle it without thinking about getting out of it or putting it off. Of all the characteristics of a successful leader, this may be the most difficult to learn.

Still another common characteristic of successful leaders is their ability to generate enthusiasm among their people. This enthusiasm projects itself from the leaders and catches on with their people. They, too, seem to be caught up in this willingness to work just for the sake of working and getting the task done. This ability to generate enthusiasm comes out differently in different leaders, but the results are easily definable. Their workers tackle their jobs with interest and excitement. They may even be jealous of anyone that comes around, especially those who would make light of their job or try to change what they are doing. They get satisfaction from their jobs and don't think of their work as "that miserable interlude between weekends." As we said, leaders may differ in how they project this enthusiasm, but the results are there nevertheless. Most likely the leaders don't have what is sometimes thought of as enthusiasm—the running-around-and-shouting kind. It isn't the back-slapping or hand-shaking thing that some do and call it enthusiasm. It can best be described as an *intense-ness that is contagious.*

A final common characteristic among good leaders is the willingness to accept responsibility. In fact, good leaders become very bored when there is little or no responsibility connected with what they are doing. They aren't afraid to accept the challenge of doing something that has risk to it. They are willing to take on a job that may allow them to fail, providing it also allows them the opportunity to succeed. They may even go out and look for responsibility if they don't get it otherwise. Instead of waiting for someone to give them the authority to do something, they will probably be pushing the top of the responsibility ladder. If they get called on the carpet, it will be for taking on too much responsibility, not too little.

**Communicating**  In Chapter 5 we discussed the subject of communication in great depth, so we suggest that the reader go back and read this again to get a refresher on the subject, this time keeping in mind that effective communication is an important characteristic of leadership. There are a few points that need to be mentioned here, though, that were not mentioned earlier.

When we can get a specific message across to another person or a group *in just the way we want it to get across,* that's good communicating. Whether we are writing letters, speaking to groups or individuals, giving orders, or passing on policies, we haven't ended our responsibilities until the message is received *and understood.* Whenever we hear ourselves saying, "Don't you remember, I told you . . ." we can be sure we have just indicted ourselves as poor communicators. We have said to the receiver, "It's your problem, not mine!"

The best single measure of our ability to communicate is to see whether what we said produced the results we were trying to get. After all, that's the usual reason for communicating, anyway—to get some kind of action. The best sign that the message has gotten through successfully, then, is to see if the policy is being carried out, or if people are coming in on time, or if they are responding in a way that indicates that they really understand what has been said.

One final word about good communicating: Not just an asset, it's a *requirement* of the job. Supervisors must accept the responsibility for what they communicate. They cannot leave it up to those on the receiving end. They cannot blame their subordinates for not getting the message; they must see that their subordinates get it even if it means doing the communicating all over again. And just as important as all the rest, they must work just as hard to communicate up the line as down. Their own bosses and those bosses up the line must manage as well as they can on the basis of the information they get from below.

**Motivating**  Motivation is a little different from leadership in that leadership inspires people to work for external reasons—often for the leader—while motivation gets them to work for internal reasons—because they want to, regardless of how they feel about the boss or the organization. Motivation is probably the single most important aspect of the supervisor's job. We can't *make* the employees work for very long and expect a good job from them. The desire to work must come from within the individual if it's going to last. But now we have a problem, because it's the specific responsibility of supervisors to see that the workers feel this way about their job—that they *want to work*. This means that we can't just say, "Well, it's not my fault. They just don't want to work." When we say that, we are openly admitting we're doing a bad job of supervising. This doesn't mean that we won't run into this problem, it just means that we have to accept the responsibility of correcting it.

In order to motivate our people, we have to understand why people work in the first place, and what it is that makes them work harder or keeps them from working as hard as they can. Of course, the basic needs are, as they have always been, for food, clothing and shelter, and safety. But once these needs have been satisfied, people still have certain *social* needs that must be met, and they are motivated when they see a chance to meet these needs. For instance, they want to be accepted by their fellow workers. They want to think that they are liked and that others want to have them around. In short, they want to be an accepted part of the work group. Supervisors must recognize this and make every effort to help the workers feel that they are a part of the organization and that the other workers respect their work. We can even do this purposely, by reflecting any favorable remarks we hear. "By the way, Charlie liked it very much because I gave you this assignment . . ." Very few successful leaders have gotten that way by sowing discord and suspicion among their workers.

Another need the workers have is for *self-esteem.* This is related to what we just said, in that people like to think that the job they are doing is important and that they are good at it. It's hard for any of us to get motivated over a job that has been downgraded and specified as not really amounting to much as far as the organization is concerned. That's why people worry about titles and having their names on the door or being in the official directory. They like people to know that they are important enough to the organization to be recognized for it. Such little things as putting name plates on the desks often will go a long way toward meeting these needs. But employees want to feel that other workers respect them for their ability to do the job. They want others to think that what they do is important, and they like to think that others look up to them just a little for their ability. But when we come along and ridicule any employee in front of the other workers, we not only put that employee in an embarrassing position, we also destroy the self-esteem that is so important to him or her. That's the main reason why we are always told to *correct in private, approve in public.*

In discussing these three points—leading, communicating, and motivating—we haven't meant to imply that we should "baby" employees. It is just common sense to recognize that certain things cause workers to work better, and that we should take advantage of these things. This is simply a calculated effort to get best results from the individuals who work for us. After all, we expect those individuals to give their machinery the proper care and maintenance; how could we possibly do less for them? It is our way of getting employees to work because they *want* to, not because they *have* to. In the end, the results are better for the organization, for the supervisor, and certainly for the employees themselves.

## CONTROLLING

While directing is the most difficult function, controlling is perhaps the most *critical*. When we plan, organize, and direct, there is still the problem of controlling all of what we have planned, organized, and are directing. Without the proper controls, all the effort may be wasted. Essentially, supervisors control three things or a combination of them, namely money, material, and people. The problem is that each is handled differently; each takes a different skill. We find it easier to budget money and materials because they are usually quite constant. Money will buy just so much and we have just so much money, so the decision is what to do with what we have. But people aren't that easy to budget; they aren't all alike and even a single individual may show different qualities from one time to another. While a dollar is a dollar, a worker isn't a worker. Replace one secretary with another and things can be quite different from when we had the first one. When we start to budget (control) people, we have to take into consideration that they work at a different speed in the morning than in the afternoon; their attitudes and behavior may be a lot different on Monday than on Friday.

Controlling is most closely related with planning, which simply says that we must have something to control. Oftentimes we may find ourselves trying to control when we actually haven't got a plan to follow. The plan serves as the *standard* against which we control, so without the plan we are doing some guess work with our controlling. For example, when we decide in the middle of an operation that the cost is getting out of hand and start to "control," we really aren't measuring this against a preset standard (or plan), so it isn't completely correct to say we are practicing the function of control. If we had planned correctly and started our controlling as soon as the plan went into effect, things wouldn't have gotten out of hand in the first place. A rule of thumb (which is not really a rule but a guide) says that when we find ourselves in a drastic action with people, materials, or money, either the planning or the controlling stage broke down somewhere.

### Steps in controlling

We generally think of controlling as consisting of three steps:

1. Determining standards
2. Measuring results against standards
3. Taking remedial action as necessary

As we have said, the plan is the standard, but here we are talking about something more specific. We are looking for the answer to certain basic questions. We need to know who sets the standards and how we will know that they are the standards. The plan may or may not have specified how far off the standards we can get without being in trouble. That is information we must have; we cannot hope to control without it. Another thing we need to know about the standards is who will measure the results of our work and who will see the results of those measurements. Is there a quality control man who reports to headquarters or do we have someone on our staff who has the partial responsibility for watching quality?

Of utmost importance is the question of what will be measured. Why is this particular thing being measured? Are we really getting valid information or are we just watching a meaningless figure? For example, do we fill out forms that tell how many magazine subscriptions are held by the office, while we just disregard the cost of rearrangements of walls and other partitions? The point here is that we must be controlling the right things or the controlling effort will go for naught. Along the same line, we may find ourselves controlling something to death. If we have two people assigned full time to watch for flaws or rejects that aren't really that costly, we are in fact "driving a tack with a sledgehammer." We sometimes discover ourselves *over*reacting to situations. The boss says to watch out for certain problems or expenditures, and we set up a control system much more complicated than is really needed. Long after the crisis is past, forms are still being filled out and reports being sent up the line. Once forms and reports come into being, it's very difficult to get rid of them. *Start them only under extreme need!*

What are some of the items that may be measured? Obviously we want to measure output of goods or services. How long did it take to provide the service or turn out the product? How much money did it take? What was the final quality and how many did we actually produce? Then we need to look at expenses closely. When we measure expenses, we must measure *all* of them. Are we taking into account everything that is being charged to the particular job? Are we considering staff help, hidden costs, load factors, and other costs that will eventually have to be accounted for?

Another thing we must account for is the use of resources. Again we're talking about people, time, and money—but this time in a little different light. Here the question of measurement is one of efficient use. Are we doing a good job of matching people and jobs? Remember, it isn't necessarily proof of good supervision if the job gets done well. We must consider who's doing the job. If our people are capable of doing much more because of experience, education, or natural talent, we can't be too proud of the fact that the job is done well. The trick is to match ability and job requirements as closely as possible, then let the people grow out of their jobs as they develop. As supervisors we must constantly measure—at least in our minds—how well the employee is matched to the job, as well as whether he or she has outgrown it.

All of this is true for the other resources we have. Are we really getting the most out of our overtime? Are we doing some jobs that could be left undone or eliminated altogether, then using time and money on overtime to do essential things? We get trapped sometimes by saying that we have to go into overtime to do a very important job, failing to realize that we got into this situation simply because we failed to control our time properly. We spent valuable time at unimportant things, forcing ourselves into overtime. The same objection applies to using people on nonessential details when they could be doing things that *must* be done sooner or later. It's all right for everyone to pitch in and help, but if this pitching in means that we must neglect other work that will get us behind schedule or cost us time and money later on, then we've made a bad decision.

### Using the budget to control

Perhaps the oldest and best control device we have is the budget. We complain about it and even wish we didn't have it, but we should be glad that there is something as rigid as the budget to guide us in our controlling. Very few organizations could run very smoothly without a budget because it gives us one of the best standards we could ask for. It gives us not only something to measure our progress by, but also something to aim at. As we constantly compare ourselves with the budget, we are also getting feedback on where we can expect to end up at the end of the budget period. Here is a means of measuring even the small parts of the job, because budgets are made up of parts. Good budgets are made up of *accurate* parts; bad budgets are made up of *padded* parts. This isn't the place to go into detail on the budget, but let's notice a thing or two about it. First of all, it is put together to let the organization know just how much money there is and where the best places to spend it are. Good budget planning takes into account local needs, and those putting it together will solicit help from all levels

in determining the best use of all the money. The trouble comes when each level starts to be unrealistic about its needs. When each group, department, or division adds just a little, by the time the total budget is drawn up there is either too big a demand or the organization finds itself looking for more money than it really needs. When this happens, the fate of most budgets is that someone at the top starts to whittle down the figure and everyone gets hurt. "But if I don't raise my figure, I'll get hurt, because they will probably make an across-the-board cut!" Even if this is so, that's a management decision and doesn't give us the right to pad our figures just because everyone else does. We shouldn't include anything we can't substantiate, because sooner or later we will have to account for what we have asked for. If our figures won't stand the test, not only will the budget be cut, but our reputation as a super-visor will suffer. The wisest thing to do is to make a realistic budget, back it up with a good set of requirements, then let management wres-tle with the problem of cutting it if they have to. Later on, if the work isn't done because of budget problems (lack of money), we can show that we put in a legitimate request that got cut by someone else.

### Measuring results

Once we have determined the standards by which we are to control, we have to measure the results *against these standards.* Sometimes this measurement is routine—just a matter of seeing how many units were produced, how many pages were typed, how many sales were made, and so forth, then reporting the obvious results in whatever manner is provided. But not all of our evaluating is that obvious or that easy. Sometimes we find ourselves in situations in which there are so many contributing factors that we aren't quite sure just what the results mean. It may be that the operation is too large, like a long assembly line with many feed-ins, or it may be that there are many people making different contributions to the end product—or the output may be service and that means there is the customer to consider. How can we measure in circumstances like this?

One of the best avenues open to us is the process known as *sampling*. There isn't anything complicated about it. It's just a means of looking at large or complicated operations and getting reliable results without having to get a measurement on every detail and every person doing work on the project. We simply look at a small, average sample and take the results to represent the entire operation. Another way to accomplish the same thing is to take one complete operation out of several, assuming that all the rest are like this one. Actually, with a little help, we can do a pretty good job of sampling and get very reliable results. Once we get in the habit of doing this, we are on the lookout for ways of getting true samples all of the time. We check the absentée list on random occasions and see if particular individuals or a particular number are absent. We spot-check three or four days in a row and see just how much time our workers are taking for break or when they are coming in from lunch. We look at customer complaints once a week for several weeks and see if any one thing is beginning to give trouble. These things are good indicators of just how well we are doing, and are good means of controlling.

When sampling doesn't seem to be a very good way of measuring the results, and the measuring seems to be too difficult to do on the whole operation, there is another way that may help. This is the simple matter of finding a *substitute* measurement. For example, we can look at such things as absenteeism or tardiness and get a good idea of what the morale is in the group. If turnover is high, this may be a good substitute measurement of how much job enrichment is going on. A look at previous production records may be a good measure of how much motivation or employee morale exists in the group, providing other things are equal. The substitute may be a tangible means of measuring very intangible things, such as attitudes, job satisfaction, morale, etc.

Of course, when we are measuring one thing to look at something else, we'd better be sure the measure is accurate, which is true of any of our measurements. Even measuring such things as how well one typist is doing compared to the others in the office may not give true results. If one typist is doing simple items and the others are doing more complex things, counting the *number of pages* is a poor way of looking at results. On the other hand, one usually accurate typist doing the same simple job day-in and day-out may begin to show a high error rate because the job *doesn't* have some variety in it. The errors may indicate that the typist is getting less satisfaction than previously. It might be the same for a salesperson. We need to be careful in evaluating one salesperson's results against another's until we are sure the territories are the same. It's all right to measure sales as a means of determining how good a salesperson is, providing we know what other salespeople in the same or similar territories have done. If a salesperson isn't doing as well as he or she should, what is the potential in that territory? Is the competition getting stronger? Does the salesperson really know the new line? Has he or she had the proper training—the same kind of training as the other salespeople? In other words, is our measurement really accurate in all respects? If so, then it becomes a good control device; if not, it becomes a dangerous tool to use in making decisions.

### Remedial action

Controlling would be useless if it didn't include the final facet of control—taking remedial action when it is required. While controlling shouldn't be thought of as just this aspect, it certainly includes it. When things are shown by our measuring processes to be running along smoothly, then we should be good enough supervisors to recognize this and leave things alone. But when the results show that the situation is getting out of hand or that we should really be doing better, then we need to know enough to step in and take some action. We may not be the ones to take the action, but we may be the ones to instigate it. As obvious as it seems, just knowing that something is wrong isn't enough; reporting it to the right people is important. If we have found that a problem exists somewhere in the group, we should ask ourselves: who really needs to know this? The answer should be: someone who can do something about it. Whether it's an overtime problem, a union grievance, or what have you, telling the right person as soon as possible may head off a much more serious problem later on.

When it comes to determining who the right person is, perhaps the worst thing we can do is say, "It's not my problem." Remember, it's our problem as soon as we hear or know about it, and it's our problem until something is done about it, or someone else takes over the responsibility for the problem. When our boss says, "O.K., I'll take over now," then we have done all we can, even if we don't like what he or she is doing.

Another important part of notifying the right person at the right time is to do it in the right way. And that doesn't mean to give him or her a telephone call just at quitting time and report the bare details. If that person doesn't get the importance of the problem, or misses some of the details, we've got to accept the responsibility for the poor results that come from improper control. The best approach is to put the problem in writing, which not only puts the information in permanent form but also provides a record that we spotted the weakness and made an effort to get it controlled. But this latter reason is secondary to the first one. It's no justification to report something just to protect ourselves. If this becomes our prime reason for acting, we aren't likely to do a very thorough job of reporting the facts; neither will we work at organizing our material, making sure what we say is clear, readable, etc.

Finally, let's repeat what was said earlier: It's a lot better to solve the problem ourselves than to pass it on to someone else. This means we must have the authority to take the necessary remedial action. It also means we may have to go through the entire planning, organizing, and directing functions all over again. If that's what the remedial action requires, being a good supervisor means doing it that way, rather than just closing our eyes to reality and going ahead toward eventual poor results.

## CONCLUSION

There are two parts to planning: planning the work and working the plan. We can't say which one is the more important. We can only say that unless each is done well, the results will suffer drastically. We've seen that getting the work done takes both directing and controlling. We have to emphasize that directing the people under us is well-named: *directing.* In many ways, we're neither leading nor pushing: *we're pointing the way.* Since our job as supervisors is to see that others do the work, we demonstrate our best directing not by our visibility "out in front of the troops" or screaming orders from the throne, but by motivating, encouraging, helping others do the work *because they want to.* The successful supervisors are the ones who direct by getting the people to believe in the job, not the boss. (It's all right to believe in the boss, but that alone shouldn't be the reason they work.) If we really are looking to be a success at supervising, we have to give up the idea that only *born leaders* make good supervisors; we have to understand that supervision is simply a long list of well-done skills, each of which can be learned. Directing people is one of those important skills!

Controlling is the least exciting and perhaps the most critical of the skills required in getting the job done. It's a matter of knowing what's going on and knowing it soon enough and well enough to do something about it before it's too late to correct the direction things are taking. It takes attention to details. It takes looking at records. It means knowing for sure what we expect and seeing how close we come to those expectations. It means that we have to have a certain amount of flexibility and "agility" at moving fast to correct a bad situation. It's the last chance we have to correct poor planning and poor directing. If we're good enough at it, we can turn even a bad situation into one that gets the job done.

## EXERCISES

1. Individual exercise: Each person should think of a person they have working for them now, or have had in the past, or one they know who is considered to have a bad attitude. They should think of a *specific* person, not just people in general who have bad attitudes. Thinking of that specific person, they should now decide *why* they say the person has a bad attitude. Make a list of the reasons.

2. Group activity: In front of the group, make a list of all the things that have been said to show that the person from exercise 1 has a bad attitude. When there is a long list, rejoin the group. Now have the group decide how many of the things listed are observable and how many of them couldn't be seen by someone standing around watching the people being discussed. (The point of this is to show that what we consider a "bad attitude" is most often poor performance. If that's the case, we don't try to change the attitude but rather the performance.)

3. Individual activity: Let each person pick a manager they have high regard for *as a manager* and write down the characteristics of that person that explain why he or she was chosen. When this is over, list these characteristics in front of the group, without calling any names of the managers chosen. See how many of the characteristics were the same. Begin to make an overall list of characteristics of good managers. Save this list.

4. Individual activity: Let each person think of a great leader they have admired, and that they know a little about. These leaders may be of the past like Napoleon or Lincoln, or they may be modern, like Golda Meir. After picking a *specific person,* list the characteristics of that person that made him or her a great leader. When the individuals have completed their list, again collect this data without listing the names of the leaders. Come up with a list of characteristics that great leaders have in common. Save this list.

5. Group activity: Now compare the two lists from exercises 3 and 4 above. There's a good chance that the lists aren't very similar, though there will be some similarity, of course. From your comparison, decide whether we are looking for the same thing when we talk about a supervisor (or manager) and a "leader." We might go a step further and ask how some of the leaders we picked would have made out as managers in our organization, especially at lower levels.

6. Group activity: Brainstorm all of the ways the organization has of getting information that allows it to "control" the activities of the organization. Which of these are supplied by the first level of supervision? Could we do a better job of supplying this information? Are there any of these reports or forms that we dread filling out or supplying? Why?

# 8
# MOTIVATING BY ENRICHING THE JOB

Motivation has long been a subject of discussion among supervisors and those who provide supervisory training. Obviously we want our people to be motivated. If they are, then they will work harder, be more pleasant, and enjoy their jobs more—with the result that they get more work done and make our job easier. A worthy goal, but one that puts a lot of responsibility on motivation, and difficult to reach *if we aren't sure how to motivate our people.*

## WHY DO PEOPLE WORK?

In order to understand how to motivate people on the job, it's necessary to find out why people work in the first place. But the question goes deeper than that because what we really want to know is what gives people the most satisfaction. If we find this out, then we know what makes them work and even what will make them work harder.

Those who have studied the matter in great detail have found out some interesting things about why people work. At first it would seem that everyone works to make money. "Stop paying me and you'll see why I'm working!" someone says, and we almost fall for it until we realize that if we made typists stand up and type all day, they'd probably quit pretty quick. By this line of reasoning, people work *so they can sit down.* We could follow the same line about benefit plans, treatment from the boss, etc. The point is, people do expect to get paid, they enjoy the things money can bring, and they like to make more money. But they don't work just for money.

Primarily, people do what they do to meet certain needs or to get satisfactions. People worry about their families' security, so they work to take care of this need. Food, clothing, and shelter are problems for any worker, so these are strong *motivating* factors. People also like to be liked. They like to have friends and loved ones who care about them and who show their feelings for them. Here again, the average worker doesn't come to the job to satisfy this need; it is met outside the job.

## A higher need

But most of us have other needs that can be met on the job. In fact, they must be met before the employee is truly motivated. We all like to have our egos "uplifted." We like to think we are useful. We like to contribute something for which we get the credit. This is a need that comes to the forefront time and again in all of us, and is the one factor that a supervisor can always depend on for use in motivation.

For a long time supervisors tried to motivate their people by making the work location a pleasant place. Often better lighting was installed, along with effective climate control for heating and air conditioning. In many cases music and flowers and artistic decor were added. Supervisors were even trained in human relations, so they would know exactly how to handle the employees that worked for them. Supervisors practiced being pleasant to their people and many tried extra things like giving time off with pay, and excused absences. Companies developed other benefits besides hospitalization and retirement plans. They provided tuition for employees who wanted to continue going to school, and sometimes scholarships for the employees' families. Surely with all these benefits, in addition to attractive wages and vacation plans, the employees were motivated almost out of control. *But they weren't.*

There is an interesting thing about the benefits mentioned above. If workers in one area have them, those who don't have them will be dissatisfied, perhaps even lack motivation. But the presence of such benefits seldom produces motivation over a prolonged period. There is no evidence to show that day in and day out any employees work hard because of a good hospitalization plan. Even when employees get an increase in wages, it rarely motivates them on a permanent basis. So do we do away with all of these things because they don't motivate employees? Obviously not, because their absence will do a great deal of harm, even if their presence doesn't serve to motivate greatly.

## THE KEY TO MOTIVATION

If none of these things motivate people to work hard over a long period of time, what's left for the supervisor to do? Actually the situation is simple, although carrying it out is pretty hard. *The job itself* holds the key to motivation. The job is the one thing that can provide employees with the satisfaction they need to be motivated. They want a chance to succeed; they want recognition; they want to feel that they have a chance to advance; they want to feel that they are making a contribution to the organization. All the benefit plans in the world will not provide these satisfactions. Only the work can do it.

But there is a potential danger here: *The job can also prevent these needs from being met.* The new supervisor may fall into the trap that many older ones are in now. We may fail to use the *job* as the best means of motivating our workers. In fact, when we take over our assignment from the last supervisor who had it, we may find that the motivating factors have been removed. If we just go along doing what the last person did, we may miss a great opportunity to provide motivation, get more work done, and look good in the process. Now let's see how it works.

Remember, we are looking for ways in which the employees' desire for recognition, achievement, chance for advancement, etc., can be satisfied right on the job. (We'll see in a minute how some employees meet these needs off the job.) We need to look at the total assignment we have given our employees and see what there is about it that will meet these needs. There are several steps we can go through to analyze the job; let's take them one at a time.

First, are jobs clearly defined? Do the employees (and do we) know exactly what is expected of them? Have we taken the time to go over each detail with each individual to be sure that he or she understands what is and what isn't his or her responsibility? What about the interfaces between employees or departments? Does each employee know where his or her job stops and someone else's starts? Are there gaps or overlaps in the assignments? We're talking about more than just a brief job description; we're talking about a comprehensive look at the job duties of each individual. Some jobs are fairly clearcut, of course, and don't require much effort to analyze. Others have some complexities about them that require a careful look to determine exactly where the boundaries are between responsibilities.

Next, we should see if there are any parts of the job that could be done at a lower level because they require less skill than the others do. Are we asking salespeople to type their own reports, secretaries to do miscellaneous filing that file clerks could do, or skilled lathe operators to sweep the aisles? Sometimes these things are best done by people with higher capabilities, but they rarely motivate those people or give them much of a feeling of accomplishment. The way to measure these kinds of things is to ask ourselves, "Does it really take that person's talent to do that part of the job?" Naturally there are some things in every job that are below the skills level of the employee doing it, but the important thing is to see just how much of the *total* time is spent on these things, and how much on those requiring more skill, judgment, experience, etc. If the lesser jobs are using up very much of the time, then they should be removed or a different individual should be placed on the job, if possible.

The next step is to look at where an employee's work comes from and where it goes when he or she is through with it. Too often employees find themselves taking work from some other person or department, doing some operation, then passing it on to someone else. Nowhere in the whole operation does anyone have any real responsibility or accountability. No one is a part of either the beginning or the end of the job.

## THE SUPERVISOR'S RESPONSIBILITY

We need to look at our own actions, too, in trying to enrich the job. Are we still doing part of the job that should be done by those under us? There is a better-than-average chance that if we came to our job from the one below us, *we're still doing more of our old job than we should.* Just because we're good at it doesn't justify not training someone else to do it. The real test of our supervisory skill is to see if we can quickly divorce ourselves from doing those things that others are paid to do, and tackle those things that *we* are paid to do.

It doesn't come easy. We all look for satisfactions in and from our jobs. Since supervision is a hard job and the responsibilities sometimes aren't exactly clear, we tend to get frustrated early in our supervisory career. Trying to overcome this frustration often leads us to find satisfaction in working with *things* instead of *people*. This means we may start working on the machines every once in awhile, stuffing envelopes, doing our own filing, anything to get a little satisfaction of accomplishment. But we should remember: Every time we do these things, we're admitting a little bit of failure. We're trying to enrich our jobs at the expense of those under us who should be doing these things.

Supervisors have to look for things that will enrich the jobs under them, even if it means reorganizing the work or shifting responsibilities. They have to recognize that not every job can be enriched, nor can every employee accept an equal amount of responsibility. Each employee has to *earn* the right to whatever responsibility is added to his or her job. Too often, we get the process backwards; we give the responsibility when employees haven't shown a willingness to accept it.

We hope that in doing this we will motivate them. But under these circumstances they may see our action as increasing their *work* rather than their responsibility. We do better to reward the acceptance of responsibility. Note the difference between the following two approaches:

"John, up until now I've been handling this. From now on I'm making it your responsibility."

"John, since you've been making the decisions on this already—and I've just been signing it—from now on would you like to send it out directly without my looking at it?"

In the first case it sounds like more work, even a little bit of a threat. In the second case it comes out as a reward for achievement, a recognition of acceptable performance, and an opportunity John doesn't have to take if he doesn't want to.

## AVOID "MORE WORK"

One of the reasons for rewarding acceptable performance is that when we begin to reorganize the work we are likely to do it along the lines of each individual's capabilities, rather than according to our own thoughts and ideas. The problem comes when we look at a job and say, "I need to give this person more responsibility," then assign more of the *same kind of work* he or she is already doing. What we have done is enlarged or expanded the job, not enriched it. (Having to dig a *wider* or *longer* ditch rarely motivates! Selecting *where* to dig the ditch just might, however.)

## PROTECT MOTIVATION

Strangely enough, if we try to motivate our people by giving them more responsibility, we may find that we have left ourselves wide open for criticism. Suppose, for example, that our secretary, Linda, does a great job of answering certain types of inquiries. Her knowledge of the subject is excellent, as is her judgment. We realize that she is only checking with us as a matter of routine. She makes the right decision, clears it with us, then handles the matter to completion. But there are times when we are out of the office or otherwise tied up, and action stops until we are able to give our approval.

Here is an excellent chance to enrich her job. We see she has earned the right to make her own decisions and to handle the matter without our even being involved. So we offer her the recognition of doing the entire thing without our approval. If she agrees, all evidence points to her doing an even better job, because it really is *her* job now.

But now a problem arises. Unless those above us are in agreement with what we are doing, we may get into hot water. Everything goes fine as long as she makes the *right* decision, but what happens when something goes out that is wrong or is contrary to policy? When we are called in by those above us to explain the action and reason for the error, we have a choice of blaming Linda or accepting the blame ourselves. It may not be enough to say, "I was trying to motivate her," because the obvious question then is, "Why does she need motivating? I thought she was a good employee."

It's just as bad to say, "I've been letting her make those decisions because when I'm out of the office, there's no one to give the approval." The response to that could be, "Maybe you're falling down on *your* job by being away too much." The whole point of this is that there are some risks involved in giving recognition to those who have demonstrated their ability to achieve. It really cannot succeed unless those above us are aware of the principles involved and agree to go along with our efforts. The worst thing that could come out of this is for our boss to say, "This nearly got us into trouble, so from now on I want you to check everything that goes out." By the same reasoning, our boss could justify checking everything we do, and having his or her boss check everything he or she does, and so on up the line. Once such edicts are issued, they are difficult to remove.

## PRODUCTION-MINDED MANAGEMENT

It really wouldn't be right to leave a chapter on motivation—where we've spent so much time talking about how we can enrich the job, how we can do things for the employees to motivate them, and how much responsibility we have as supervisors to enrich their jobs—without putting in something on *production.* When it comes right down to it, getting out the work or the service is what it's all about. It's why there are employees and why there are supervisors. Even charitable organizations don't exist just to keep the employees on the payroll, for the most part. Hospitals and service organizations have to give good service. They have to think about saving money. Any nonprofit organization can exist only so long as its directors feel that the service being given is up to the standard of expectation for the amount of budget it takes to offer that service. Profit-centered organizations understand this at management levels. It may not be understood at lower levels. Even first-line supervisors may be so closely tied to the working units that they miss the point that production is the reason there is any profit at all.

We have to understand that "saving money" and "making a profit" *aren't bad words.* And they *aren't bad reasons* for working effectively. Whatever style the supervisor finally develops as his or hers, it must take into account that if the employees don't produce (whatever the reason), something will have to be done. This doesn't suggest that we aren't interested in the employee and that we don't try hard to provide means of motivation. In fact, it means just the opposite. We do all of these things because we've seen that they produce motivated workers and motivated workers produce more. It does suggest, though, that the supervisor must keep in mind that just making the employee happy on the job or making the organization a good place to work isn't the end of the matter. The employees should understand this, too. The end of it all is to get the most production from the fewest people with the best product or service that we can offer. In a profit-making organization, it also means making it better and/or cheaper than the competition.

What do we do as a result of this knowledge of the need for production? We watch the results in terms of production, *not employee satisfaction alone.* If we believe the idea that people are likely to respond with more production when they believe in the job, then we do whatever we can to enrich their jobs and make them meaningful and show how the jobs contribute to the overall scheme of things. We'll also watch production figures and job standards and see if we're on target. We'll see how many calls the sales force is making; we'll see how many cases are handled; we'll see how many usable parts are coming off the line; we'll see how many customers are being waited on. We'll pass this information on to the employees as their *reason for being there.* We'll also show our dissatisfaction when we continually fall short of the goals that are reasonable to meet.

Finally, we have to understand that the first-line supervisor is closer than anyone else in the organization to the major causes—and the means of prevention—of inflation. To see this, we have only to recognize the typical inflationary pattern:

Wages increase.

Cost of materials increases.

Time to produce a product or service remains the same or increases.

Production of product or service increases slightly or not at all.

When these four elements exist—and it doesn't always take all four of them—we have inflation. That means we have to pay more for the same thing. And that means we go back to our employer and ask for a "cost-of-living" increase. And *that* means it's going to cost our employer *more* to provide the *same* service or product. So ... prices will have to be raised, and the spiral will continue. It will always continue under these circumstances until one thing happens: *Production goes up*—and far enough to offset the increased costs. If we get more production for the same amount, we can even *lower* the price and the users of the service or product can get more for their money instead of less. This is the way to stop inflation. The new supervisor, especially at the first level, has to constantly think of ways to get more production from the same people, or get the same production at lower cost—or both. An alternative would be to improve the product or service, so that when the customer pays more, he or she gets more for the money. But this may often prove a poor alternative to just holding down the cost of a product or service that has already proven satisfactory.

## CONCLUSION

As we suggested in the last chapter, when we were talking about directing people, leadership in the world of supervision is different from the rest of the world's idea of leadership. So is motivation. Many think that to motivate people is to stir them up to the point where they go charging out and work themselves into exhaustion, just because their leader has inspired them so much. In supervision, the idea is to get them involved in fulfilling enough of their own needs through the things the job offers so that they get satisfaction from doing the job. When the job is challenging enough, meaningful enough, and gives enough recognition, supervisors don't have to offer *any* motivation. The supervisors' job is to make sure the job offers all those things. There's not much that will motivate a person more than having responsibility for some specific tasks that are well-defined and *well-recognized as necessary.* But not everyone deserves or can take responsibility. It should be given as a reward—and only when those it's offered to agree to take the consequences of failure as well as the rewards of success. This means the employees must have the *right to make mistakes,* to be wrong, as well as the right to be right. It means that when we give responsibility as a way of creating motivation, we can't check everything that goes out and correct the errors. If we check everything, we've only left the employee the *right to be right.* If errors are stopped by us, the employee will never have to live with the mistakes—and the consequences of those mistakes. If the employee knows he or she will have to live with consequences, the end result is an employee who works much harder *at being right* and who is, in fact, motivated.

## EXERCISES

1. Individual activity: Let all of the participants think about themselves in their present jobs. Each should write down what makes a good day for him or her right now. Think of at least three situations in the last week where motivation has been high—so high that the person has thought about the activity before coming to work, and was anxious to get to work and get into it. After each has listed at least three situations, let them go back and analyze each one and see what it was that made the job exciting or motivating for them. Think of the characteristics of the job, not the actual activity. When all have finished, record the information for future use.

2. Group discussion: Looking at the list from exercise 1 above, decide how many of these items could be built into any job, even nonsupervisory ones. See how many of the things were common with everyone. Is it possible that we could motivate our people with the same kinds of things?

3. Individual activity: Let each person think of one employee who is usually very motivated to do the job assigned. Carefully analyze the *job* that employee is doing, and the way we make the assignment. See if we can figure out just what it is that motivates the employee on the job. See if it's possible that something about the job motivates the employee, rather than his or her own attitude. (It's not enough just to say, "Anything I ask that person to do makes him or her excited." We also have to see how much responsibility we've given the person, and how we make the assignment.) Record the results of the whole group, and save the information for further use.

4. Group activity: Analyze the "motivation factors" given in the last exercise. Are there any common factors? Would any of them motivate us? Are they similar to the ones found in exercises 1 and 2? Now the critical question: Would the same approach work for all of our employees?

5. Individual activity: Let each person think of one employee who

usually is not in the least motivated. Carefully analyze the *job* the person is doing and the way we make assignments to him or her. See if we can figure out if there is anything about the job that fails to motivate the person. Is it possible that the job itself isn't very motivating? Record the group's results and save for future use.

6. Group activity: Analyze the characteristics given in exercise 5. Throw out the ones that are not measurable, like "The employee is just plain lazy," and deal only with those that have to do with the nature of the job or the way the assignment is given. See if there is anything about the job that fails to motivate. If we were working for this supervisor and had this work to do, and had this amount of responsibility, would *we* be motivated?

# 9
# INTERVIEWING SKILLS

When we talk with people about specific things, such as telling them how they are doing on the job, or correcting some fault in their work performance, or trying to assist them in solving some personal problem they may have, we call this *interviewing*. This is one more technique the new supervisor needs to learn, and the more we do it the better we should get at it. The problem is, though, that we don't really do very much interviewing from day to day, so even experienced supervisors get rusty in the procedures. The best thing we can do is to look at the techniques required, practice them whenever we can, think about each interview we conduct, and bone up on the techniques each time we have another interview.

In this chapter we will talk about the general principles of conducting any kind of interview, then look at some specific kinds, namely Employment, Counseling, Disciplinary, Appraisal, and Exit. As we have said, interviewing is not an everyday occurrence for the supervisor, so we can't really expect to be experts in the subject, but since there are some basic points we can remember, it's good to look at them every once in a while. We name them so we can talk about them separately, but actually we find ourselves combining them at times, as we will see in the discussion.

## GENERAL PRINCIPLES

Basically there are three general purposes of an interview: to *predict behavior*, as in the case of an employment interview, where we want to know how well we think the employee or potential employee will do on a job; to *change behavior* where it isn't meeting a standard, such as the disciplinary interview when the employee is tardy or below production standard or has an attitude that is affecting the behavior of others; or to *establish exactly what the behavior is,* as in the appraisal interview. When we are preparing for an interview—and let's hope we always do prepare before we have one—we need to decide which of the purposes we have in mind for it. Why are we having it, why are we having it now, and why are we having it with this particular person? But we need to establish not only why we are doing this, but also *what we hope to accomplish* in the interview. If the purpose is to change behavior, do we know what the specific behavior is that we want, or do we just not like the way the person is doing now? It's pretty embarrassing to tell the person, "I don't like the way you're doing now, but I can't tell you what I'd like you to to be doing." Once we've decided what we don't like and what we would prefer, we need to know how we are going to get the person to change. And we should know whether we expect the total change to be made as a result of this interview, or whether there will be more later.

The best thing to do before an interview is write these things down on a piece of note paper. We don't need to be elaborate. We just write ourselves a note stating the purpose of the interview, where we're going, why we're going there, and how we expect to get there. This has the great advantage of making us organize our thoughts whether we like to or not. It may even convince us that this is not the time to have the interview, or that we need to talk to all of our people, or that we need more information, or that we should have had the interview earlier. At least it will give us an opportunity to spend a few moments analyzing the situation before we get into it, which is always helpful.

### Establishing the proper climate

Let's emphasize something we said earlier: interviewing is *talking with people*. We didn't say talking *to* people, or talking *at* people. We said talking *with* them. There is a difference. Talking with people means that we listen as much as we talk. It means that the other person has something to say and a right to say it. When the interview is over, we can be sure it was a bad one if our reflections show us that we did most of the talking, or if the interviewee got a lot of information from us. This tells us that we did the talking and he or she did the listening. On the other hand, we can probably say that it was a good interview if we got a lot of information, and the interviewee did a lot of the talking. So *listening* is one of the things we must determine to do.

We must determine to be *fair*. We must face up to the fact that each of us probably has prejudices that affect our thinking. Since we each see things from our own standpoint, we most likely don't see them alike. Part of deciding to be fair in our interviews is to admit that there is always the chance that the interviewees might be right. At least there is the possibility that they could be nearer right than we are. This doesn't mean that we are going against the established facts. It means that we are willing to admit that our employees have some right on their side and we are willing to hear them out. One good way to approach the interview is to try to put ourselves in the interviewees' position and view the situation from their standpoint, even if we think the situation is an extreme one. Another part of determining to be fair is deciding how we will let interviewees know we want to be that way. The best way to convince them is to *show* them, not tell them. When they say something, we listen and accept what they say. We refer to it later, to let them know that we listened. We give them a chance to defend themselves or to state more facts or disagree with us, all in a threat-free situation.

We start our interviews by letting the interviewees know that we want to talk to them under the best conditions. When they come in we greet them in such a manner as to let them know we were expecting them and are planning to talk and listen. We don't say, "Wait a few minutes until I finish these important things and I'll talk to you." While we probably wouldn't say it just that way, we can easily leave that impression by continuing to work while interviewees stand ill at ease. We greet them, and show that they come first by making sure that our calls are taken by someone else and that no one will interrupt us. We seat our interviewees comfortably, not in an awkward position where they have to turn to see us, or look around some books, or otherwise be uncomfortable. If we have room or it isn't too obvious that we don't usually do it, it's often a good idea to come out from behind our own desk and sit beside our interviewees rather than across the desk from them. Of course, if we have papers we need to refer to, then sitting behind the desk is probably the best arrangement.

Any time we are talking with people it makes good sense to open the conversation on some light topic instead of jumping abruptly to the point. Our opening remarks, then, show an interest in our interviewees, their families, their jobs, or their hobbies. This shouldn't be forced, though. It should be genuine interest. Most importantly, it shouldn't be too long. Interviewees know we want to talk to them and maybe even what it is we want to talk about, so the sooner we get to to the subject the quicker they will begin to relax. Some people like to *sneak* into the subject, but that is a dangerous way to get to the point, because we really have nothing to hide. We wanted to talk to each of these people, so we have provided the opportunity for the interview. Even if they asked for these sessions, we still shouldn't wait for them to bring up the subject. We are the supervisor—the boss—and we are in our office. It's up to us to take the lead. All of this simply means that as soon as appropriate, we start talking about the subject of the interview, without beating around the bush. "Jim, I called you in so we could go over your question about . . ." This gets us started and no one is surprised. This way Jim knows quickly what the subject is about and can get his thoughts in order. He knows why he's there, what we expect him to discuss, and can give us information without guessing. After all, we want him to be free to speak and to give us as much good, usable information as possible. This can happen only if he knows what it is we're talking about.

As we have said, the interview is as much a listening routine as a talking one for us. We give full attention to the answers to our questions. We listen when the interviewees talk. We consider their remarks, answer their questions the best we can, but keep the interview focused on the topic at hand. One of the errors most often committed is to let those being interviewed get us off the subject and cause us to discuss things that we really hadn't prepared to talk about. When our time is up we discover that we haven't covered the material we wanted to talk about, and either have to schedule another interview or make this one go longer than we intended. But if we have directed the interview properly, we should close without letting it drag on. Once we've gotten the information we wanted, answered the interviewees' questions or settled the problem, the wisest thing to do is to end the session as quickly and politely as possible. One good way for us to close and also to get a little feedback from them is to ask them to sum up the findings as they see them. This way we can see if they have any misunderstandings about the things that have been discussed and also let them know that the interview is over. If there is any action to be taken, state that plainly, as well as who will do the action:

"I'll call you Thursday."

"We'll try it for a month, then talk again."

"You call me when you've decided what you want to do about the job."

We should remember to let the interviewees leave on the same friendly note they came in on, regardless of the outcome of the interview. Even if there is a disagreement, there is no need to be disagreeable.

## THE EMPLOYMENT INTERVIEW

Often the job of interviewing new or prospective employees is not the job of the new supervisor, but it's well to know some of the techniques just the same. Even if the personnel department or someone over us makes the decision on whom to hire, we still may have to interview the individual to decide exact job placement or to give our final approval. If there is a possibility that the individual will end up working for us, we should *want* to interview the person, not try to avoid it. Let's examine why this interview is so important to us, the individual, and the organization.

Any time we add someone to our organization, we are in the process of trying to match a person and a job. Surely few things we do can affect the outcome of the job more than this. There is a good chance that we are starting someone on a career. We are saying that this person has the unique qualifications to fit the particular job, or at least the potential to grow into it. In a real way the individual is relying on us to decide whether or not he or she is suited for the job. When we ask the typical questions so often asked: "Well, do you think you will fit into this job?" or "How do you think you will like this work?" we may be asking unfair questions. If we've done our interview correctly, we are in a better position to know the answers than the applicant is. We know the job and we should know him or her pretty well by now. All of these are reasons why the interview is important from the applicant's standpoint. From the organization's standpoint it's equally important. It's much easier to get an employee on the payroll than off of it. It's much more enjoyable too! So we should do the hiring very carefully. Sometimes the organization may pass employees around from one job to another trying to find something they can do, all because they shouldn't have been hired in the first place. Whoever made the mistake in hiring them has cost the organization considerable money and wasted time. We need to be sure we do our job of interviewing carefully so this can't be said about us a few years from now. Finally, for a rather selfish reason, we need to do a good job of selecting the new employees who are going to work for us. They are going to be doing our work for us, or at least a part of it, and if they don't work out well, we aren't likely to be able to simply replace them. We will have to make them do or let the job suffer.

When we conduct employment interviews we should be certain of their purpose. Primarily, there are two basic things we want to accomplish: give information and get information. Perhaps the getting of information is the most important. What kind of information do we want to get? First, we want to get whatever past employment history we can. We need to find out what skills our prospective employees have *used,* not just which ones they have. How much growth have they shown? What kind of promotions or advancement did they have on their last job? How stable are they as employees? Does this one have a record of moving from one job to another or has he or she been on one or two for several years? Such questions as "What did you do to develop in your last assignment?" will tell us a lot if we listen carefully enough.

Asking questions is a good way to find out about the interviewees' attitudes toward supervision, too. Is this one aggressive, not wanting to be supervised? Is that one easily disgruntled? Adaptable? "What kind of bosses do you like best?" "Tell me about some of your good supervisors." "What bothers you the most about bosses?" These aren't trick questions; the answers should give us useful information. We aren't playing games, and we should let employees know that. If one says she likes bosses that let her alone, let her make mistakes as well as get credit for what is good, then she may have the makings of an excellent employee. If another says he likes bosses to give him clear directions and keep him posted along the way, we may find that he isn't as aggressive as we would like, especially if the job is one that may require individual thinking. And if still others give us a series of stories about supervisors who didn't understand them, or who picked on them all the time, we may find that it won't be long before we fall into that same category—hearing complaints about how we pick on them!

It's wise for us to delve into the personal ambitions of employees at this time. Where do they expect to go in the organization? (Not what job, since they may not know our organization that well, but how high up do they feel their capacity for responsibility and authority might take them?) We need to know whether they're going to be willing to learn the jobs one at a time, or expect to move up very rapidly without really finding out what's going on. We should try to find out whether they will be content to work satisfactorily on one job without a promise of promotion. But we don't find out these things by just asking them. We don't say, "Do you want to learn the job before moving up?" We can ask the interviewees just how they see themselves preparing for a career. We can ask what part they think experience plays in their development. Here again, we aren't likely to get explicit answers but we will get some good indicators. Our ability to interpret the answers will grow as we get more experience, but it isn't as hard as it might sound. *The key is still our ability to listen.*

The second major purpose of the employment interview is to *give* information. Prospective employees need to know something about the organization, *but not everything.* They need to know about those policies, objectives, restrictions, and benefits that most affect them and apply to them. Automatic increases, bonuses, and paid vacations probably mean much more to the young single person than the sickness benefits and the retirement plan. Accomplishments of the organization, provisions for the family, and promotion opportunities mean much to the mature person looking for a career. But this isn't the place to oversell the organization. While we don't have to accentuate the weaknesses, we don't have to pretend the place is perfect, either. Above all, be honest, especially if interviewees ask specific questions. It's better for them to know about any restrictive policies now than to find them out later on by surprise.

Part of the reason for giving out information is to let interviewees know about the job they will be doing. Again, honesty is the rule. If there is likely to be much overtime, say so. If the job is routine at times, don't be afraid to mention it; at the same time point out the more exciting features as well. If interviewees aren't likely to understand the terminology, don't spend a lot of time going into great detail about the job. Let them ask questions after you have given them enough information to make their questions meaningful. It's even a good idea to "help" them ask questions. "Do you have any questions about the operation?" "Is there something that I can give you more information about?" A key consideration here is to be sure not to hire a person on the next job above the one he or she will be working on. To tell interviewees "After a little while you should be promoted to the next level and on that job you will be doing . . ." is a bad way to go. If they won't take the job we are offering them, we don't promise them another one as a bribe to take this one! Above all, let them know what their salary and vacation schedule are. Make it clear to them in exact terms. It is often good to even give interviewees a rough breakdown of the deductions so they won't be completely surprised if their check is less than they expected. If they aren't entitled to a full vacation with pay the first year, be sure they know it. Don't rationalize by saying they didn't ask about that. Don't leave it up to them to ask about such important considerations.

If interviewees ask about the future, we tell them to the best of our ability, but obviously we shouldn't promise them anything that we aren't sure we can deliver. Perhaps the best thing to do is let them see what others have done with backgrounds and experience similar to theirs. But since it's an interview, it's well to get their views, their ideas, their questions about the future. Find out where they see themselves going and how fast they want to get there. "Where do you think your skills and talents will best direct you in our business?" This kind of question will always give us some insight into the interviewees' hopes and aspirations. They must realize that the future depends as much on them as on the organization, so questions that will let us know how they are likely to relate to the organization and the people around them will give us more information. The questions should be worded correctly, though, or the answers won't give very meaningful information. It would be useless to ask "How did you get along with your last boss?" Anybody would be foolish to answer anything but "Fine!" If we ask "What kind of boss did you like the most?" (as we have already suggested) then we get the employees' views, not a baited answer. The same is true about asking "Do you get along with people?" That's what we want to know, but we won't find out by asking a direct question. We'll get better information if we say something like, "Tell me about some of the people you didn't get along with very well in your last job." This is a leading question, but we haven't supplied the interviewees with any clues as to the "right" answer, so they must answer from their own ideas and feelings.

## THE COUNSELING INTERVIEW

Sometimes employees have problems, and the result is that we find ourselves involved in counseling interviews. Since the problems may be of the emotional type, these interviews will differ from the others we will have. The approach will be different, too. Most often, counseling interviews come about as a result of employees coming to us, rather than our going to them. Because of this we are seen in a little different light. We don't have the same kind of controls on the time or duration, topics to be discussed, and so forth, as we do in the other types of interviews. As supervisors, we are concerned about the employees' well-being, of course, but we are also concerned with their performance. If their problems affect their performance on the job, we have to help them or resolve those problems in some way to protect the organization as well as the individual. Most personal problems are not job-related at all, but if they have a bad effect on job performance, most employees will realize it. They'll know that they aren't doing as well as they are capable of doing, and this just compounds their worries, making the original problem worse. For this reason, if it is at all possible, we should

help our employees solve whatever personal problems they bring us without any reference to job performance. Besides, this in itself may make them feel a little better and more capable of dealing with other things.

Interestingly enough, employees may not even know the real causes of their problems. They may have some family problems that cause them to come to work in a bad frame of mind, or may cause them to interpret things in the wrong light, or may even cause them to say and do things that create problems for others around them. They may have financial problems that cause them to worry and fail to concentrate on their job. Their lack of concentration may create safety problems or cut into production schedules. It may cause errors that show up much later in our operation. One of the serious consequences of employees' worrying about financial problems may be that they will get all kinds of delusions about what their salary should be, how much overtime they should get, and what kind of intervals they should have between raises. It may even affect the employees' union activities, especially if their union begins to make promises of great demands and rewards.

### Help them out

Because of the personal nature of these interviews and the fact that the employees have to come to us, we have to be very careful to treat the interviews as opportunities to *help* them, not threaten them. We shouldn't say, "I'm glad you're here. I've been wanting to talk to you." Nothing would frighten any employee off quicker. The best thing to do is simply let them know we will listen, and will let them talk. We also want to convey the idea very strongly that *we want* to help. Because the employee has come to us, this a good opportunity to get things straightened out, but we have to be careful not to mess up the chance. We have to remember that *we are not trained psychologists*! If we think we can help, we should do our best to help. If we have *any* doubts, we should very quickly refer the employee to someone who is better trained to do the counseling than we are.

As we listen to our employees and try to decide what to advise them to do, we need to face the fact that we may never get either full or accurate information from them. We may get false conclusions, conclusions based on too little information, on emotion, or on imagined facts. Because of this, we need to be careful not to make the same mistakes. We should be very careful in drawing any conclusions on our own. Probably the worst thing we can do is to form an opinion very early in the interview, then look only at that evidence which supports our opinion. But this doesn't mean that we can't recommend any action or make any suggestions. It's possible to help employees even without getting all the information we'd like. The fact that they don't go away with all their problems solved doesn't mean that their meeting was unsatisfactory. If we have provided them with the opportunity to unwind, to talk, to know that someone will actually listen and not try to regulate them, we may have gone a long way toward helping to solve the problem. If they attack the organization or policies, answer questions truthfully, but avoid being defensive. We surely want to keep from getting emotional, especially if an employee is that way. We don't want to cover up the truth about the organization, an employee's work, or our feelings toward him or her. We might do more harm than good if we tell an employee that everything is rosy, knowing all the time that we are going to have to take some serious action in the near future.

When employees come to us with problems, there are two approaches we can take, each quite different from the other. We can assume responsibility for the problems. We can take the whole load on our shoulders, look for solutions, get information for the employees, offer to go as far as we can to do whatever is necessary to solve the problems for them. As undesirable as this sounds, there are times when we would go this far. When an employee comes to us apparently at his or her wit's end, or unwilling or unable to face the problem squarely, we need to step in and give support. Obviously we don't take over permanently, but in time of stress the employee needs to know that somebody who cares also is strong enough to accept the responsibility for his or her problem. Just as obviously, we shouldn't step in and take over the problem *just because it's been brought to us*. Part of the problem may be that the employee is unwilling to recognize the problem as his or her fault and may be trying to place the responsibility on someone else. For us to step in and take over would be the worst thing to do.

The other extreme from our taking over is to let the employee take the responsibility entirely on himself or herself. We just listen. We ask some questions, end up by more or less saying "That's interesting," but doing nothing. Again, as unlikely as it seems, there are times when this is exactly the right approach. When the employee shows he or she has the strength to face the problem, but wants a sympathetic ear, we would do a lot of harm if we took over. All of us like to have someone to talk to now and then. We aren't necessarily looking for advice. We aren't even expecting the person we're talking with to agree or disagree with us. We just find that we understand our problem at the end of the conversation, and even more so if the other party happens to ask us a pertinent question or two. So it is when an employee comes to us with a problem and appears to just want to talk. Our best response is to let him or her do just that.

Ideally, of the two options, the one that allows the employees to take the responsibility for their problems is the best. Even if we start off by taking over, we should also immediately begin to look for ways to return the responsibility to them. Gradually we shift it back by asking questions and letting the employees supply the answers instead of the other way around. As they begin to take the responsibility again, we keep them on the right track by asking the right questions—questions that simply make them face another truth or help them avoid the wrong conclusion—and step in only when they appear to be running out of steam. Most important of all, we should avoid trying to be the hero and get all the credit for the solution. We're looking for the credit without knowing it when we adopt the "fatherly" attitude of "I think it'll work out all right if you just take my advice." The important thing is to get the problem solved, not to get credit for solving it. The thing that may make the solution most effective is our ability to convince the employee that it was *his* or *her* solution.

Finally, keep employees' problems confidential, if possible. Avoid putting those problems into their personnel records, especially when they have come to you expecting to get private help. If there was a discussion about performance, or the meeting resulted from a performance problem, then it may be necessary to put this in the files. If appraisal records are open to other supervisors, we should be careful about putting anything about this meeting in those records unless employees are agreeable to it. Another caution is to avoid casually mentioning the problem to other supervisors. If we give up the confidence that has been given us, we not only stand to aggravate the problem, but we can be sure we've had our last counseling interview.

## THE DISCIPLINARY INTERVIEW

Counseling interviews are difficult because they are different from other types of interviews. Disciplinary interviews are difficult because they have the potential of being very unpleasant. They are one of those necessary evils that supervisors have as a part of their job. But note: the disciplinary interview is a basic requirement of our job and rarely ever is as bad as we expect it to be. The reason we have to have disciplinary interviews is that employees break rules. We have to have rules and regulations—standards of the job—but rules get broken. Not everyone meets every standard all the time. When employees fail too often or by too great a margin to meet the standard, we have to discipline them—*or change the standard.* We simply can't run an organization in which people continually fail to meet the standards set by those in position to know what a good standard is. Nothing lowers morale more quickly or destroys our effectiveness as a supervisor more completely than allowing someone to constantly break the organization's rules. If we set a precedent by letting one person get away with something, we have little chance of stopping others who decide to try the same thing. It's equally hard on the person who wants to abide by the rules when everyone else is allowed to do otherwise. Even when it's no more than one person who habitually comes in late, if the office hours are established and accepted, then everyone should abide by them; no exceptions.

When considering the disciplinary interview, the simplest way is to take a *positive* attitude toward it. For the good of all concerned, something needs to be done. If the problem is allowed to continue, nothing but trouble can result. The organization is suffering because of the situation, and to let things get worse because we dread doing something unpleasant doesn't make good sense. Not only is the organization not functioning at it's best, but our job is harder because of the problem and we, too, are failing to operate as well as we can. We are having to cover up or redo or make excuses or explain to others because of the situation that one employee has gotten us into, so we have every right to attack the problem head-on. We have already seen that the others in the group are going to become involved, especially if the situation is allowed to continue without corrective action, so for the good of the others in the work group we need to do something in a hurry. Even the employees who cause the problems suffer from them. Their careers are in jeopardy, because the longer this goes on the worse we think of them—perhaps even worse than they deserve. So, regardless of how unpleasant the interview may appear, the reasons for conducting it are real enough. If we do a good job of it and get the problem solved, we will be the stronger for it, and all concerned will be happier and better workers as a result. But two things are worthy of special note here: No matter how much we dread the confrontation, it won't get any easier if we put if off. Second, this kind of interview rarely is as bad as we expect it to be.

## The process

Disciplinary interviews begin just like the others we have talked about. Our first action is to put our interviewees at ease, going through the steps we have discussed. The worst thing we can do, of course, is jump down their throats the minute they walk into the office. If we feel that our temper is going to explode, then we'd better call off the interview until we calm down. We must continually remind ourselves that all our employees are valuable, and we mustn't do anything that will cause them to become less valuable. We aren't trying to win a battle—we're trying to get the organization back to running in the way it should be. We aren't even trying to prove any points, neither are we trying to prove that any interviewee is wrong and we are right. We are simply trying to correct a situation that cannot be allowed to continue. Our employees must know that we are trying to be fair. From the moment we begin talking to them, they must recognize this. Being fair means that we want to hear their side of the matter, and want to know any facts they might have to add to the total knowledge we have. This brings up an important point: We must have as much information as possible before we start the interview. Perhaps more than any other kind of interview, the disciplinary interview requires that we be fully informed. This certainly is no time to discover that we have our facts wrong, or that we don't have the whole story. And it's just as important to remember to have the facts substantiated. When we say, "You've been late nearly every day this month," we aren't really making a hard, factual statement. We'd do much better to have the exact information, and say, "You've been late 14 days this month." The difference between the two statements is the difference between confidence and shaky ground.

We must also be sure that the interviewees know they're being disciplined. Sometimes we catch ourselves trying to sneak the disciplinary comments in between praising comments, and the interviewees lose the message. If we wait until they're about to leave and then say, "By the way . . ." and go into the reasons for our calling them into the session, we've done both them and ourselves an injustice. They should know from the start that this is the purpose of the interview. They should know that their behavior has been unacceptable. We should tell them what the standard is and where they have failed to meet it. Just as clearly, we should let them know what corrections are expected and when they should take place. Of course, this isn't just a "tell, tell, tell" interview. As quickly as possible—when we have stated the reason for the interview—we should start to "listen, listen, listen." We want to be sure the interviewees have a chance to state their side of the question. There is always the distinct possibility that they may have some things in their favor that we haven't considered. If someone says, "My last boss told me it was all right," or, "The other departments started doing this two months ago," we'd better be prepared to study the matter further. At least we should know it, if these things are so.

Finally, we should deal with the employees' specific problems, not their total performance—unless that total performance is in question. There's little to be gained by making interviewees look worse than they really are just to prove a point. We need to be ready to admit their strengths and be willing to praise them as the occasion arises. But we can't let the good points overshadow the bad, nor can we hide the fact that they are being called to answer for their conduct. Like most interviews, the disciplinary one needs to terminate with the same preciseness with which it begins. The longer we drag it out the more danger there is that we will begin to cloud the issue. Simply put, we need to deal with the problem, state the standard, state the acceptable behavior we expect from the employee, listen to all the facts, answer pertinent questions, be sure that he or she understands what happens now—*then end the interview.* If possible, we end on a positive note of our expectations for better performance; we end on a pleasant note to show we expect things to work out; but above all, we end it.

## THE APPRAISAL INTERVIEW

When we appraise our people, we generally end up with an interview to discuss the matter with them. This is called an appraisal interview. It should be done periodically for the benefit of the employees and ourselves. They need to know their strengths and weaknesses and we need to know how they see themselves and the job. But if the organization has a regularly scheduled time for making appraisals, then we must observe this caution: we shouldn't wait until that one certain time each year to let employees know how they're doing. If we expect smooth development of the people who work for us, we must let them know as often as possible where they need to grow. *Once a year isn't often enough.* So the appraisal interview isn't something that's done once a year to satisfy some organizational policy; it's something that we do with our employees as often as we need to discuss their growth and development.

The primary purpose of the appraisal interview is to get a comprehensive look at employees as they fit into the organization, and how they will fit into it in the future. It should be one of the most enjoyable of all sessions we have with the employees, because it's a time to do what we should spend a great deal of time doing—helping employees grow. For this reason we shouldn't confuse this type of interview with the disciplinary one. This isn't the time to point out the faults of the interviewees; we don't save the disciplinary actions to bring them out at this time. The purpose of the interview should be clear in our minds, and clear to the employees. They should know why we're having the get-together and even make plans for their own activity during the interview.

### Employee participation

Employees should be given every chance to be a part of every interview, but especially this one. They should know in advance that the interview is planned. They should know that we want them to participate and that we will be talking about the *future* as well as the past. Of course, each interview starts with putting the employee at ease, but this one shouldn't take as long as the others. Most employees want to know how well we think they are doing and are anxious to get to the subject, especially if they know in advance that we want to talk about their progress. As soon as we get into the subject, we should let the employees tell us how they see themselves. It's good if they are allowed also to explain how they see their *jobs* at this same time. By doing a brief task analysis they let us know what they think their job is, which may explain why they have certain shortcomings—there may be some things they just don't know they're supposed to do. As we begin to compare our views with those of the interviewees, we need to be careful that they don't lose sight of the fact that we want them to be a part of the discussion. If we become too domineering, they'll begin to think that it doesn't really make much difference what they think—we've already got our minds made up. So we try to keep them in the conversation throughout the entire interview. We give them the honest impression that this is *their* session, their opportunity to get the facts on how they're doing and where they're going. When they see something differently from the way we see it, their opinion should be as good as ours. If they have the supporting data, then we should accept what they say. (Just because they work for us doesn't mean that they have fewer brains or are less honest.)

In the appraisal interview we should, ideally, concentrate on the future as much as possible. Even when we're talking about past performance, we want it to relate to the employees' future performance. How can they change to do things better? What are they doing now that is great and likely to enhance their chances for promotion in the future? As much as possible, we should let them set their own goals and decide what actions will produce the best results for them and the organization. Certainly they should be allowed to participate in setting objectives for themselves and selecting any corrective action that is decided on. As we look at the interviewees' future, we help them set both long- and short-range goals for themselves. The long-range ones will deal with their ambitions, their study, their direction in the organization. The short-range ones will have to do only with the job at hand. We will want to help them see that there is a certain amount of danger in looking too far ahead, especially if they begin to forget about the obligations of their present job. Too many people have lost out in the future because they didn't give enough attention to the present. Part of our obligation as a supervisor is to let the employees under us know how they are doing on their present assignment so they will have an opportunity to make the most of the future. The appraisal interview allows us an excellent opportunity to do this, especially if we let the employees be a part of setting the short- and long-range objectives for themselves.

As in any interview, we should be sure the employees know exactly what we are saying. We should state how we see their job and their future. As their interview draws to a close, we should begin to summarize and clear up any misunderstandings that have arisen. If we have decided upon some specific training or other course of action, we should state that clearly, also. If there is to be some kind of follow-up, then the time and place should be settled. Even if another meeting isn't scheduled, we should establish that we don't want to wait until next year to talk about the interviewee's progress and future. But not only should employees feel free to talk to us, they should be equally free to initiate such a meeting.

Finally, we should note that some employees may take our appraisal efforts as just another chance to criticize them. They may not accept the things that we say. They may not agree with our estimate of them. They may rationalize and blame the organization or the other members of it around them. If we do our best and the situation still turns out this way, then we have actually found out even more about these employees than we already knew. We now know that they can't take criticism, and they lack the ability to see themselves as others see them. If so, then *so be it.* We've done our part; we'll continue to do our part. We'll continue to let these employees participate in forming their future. We'll continue to let them get involved in these types of interviews. We'll even look at our own information and see if it's faulty in some way. But we must still be the supervisor and we must still hold to that which we see and believe. The worst thing we can do is to let employees bluff us into changing our minds or our actions. But the chances

of this getting to be a real problem are pretty slim. As we have said, employees want us to tell them how we see them, both in the job now and in the future. If we have done a good job of preparing for the interview, we'll be glad we conducted it, and will look forward to the next one!

## THE EXIT INTERVIEW

As new supervisors, very few of us get the opportunity to conduct exit interviews, which are simply interviews with employees who have indicated in a positive way that they want to leave the organization. The purpose of these interviews isn't to try to persuade the employees to change their minds. Often supervisors do this and end up making things worse than they were when the employees decided to leave. So why have interviews with people who are leaving, especially if we aren't supposed to talk them into staying with the organization?

The reasons are pretty obvious when we start to think about all the things we can learn from such interviews. As supervisors we need to check our perception. How well do we know the individuals who are leaving? Do we really know why they're leaving? Do we really know what their relationship with the rest of the organization is? The answers to these questions should come out of the interviews—to check our perception. Another reason for exit interviews is to check our own abilities as supervisors. Have we got some weaknesses that could be corrected? Are we somehow at fault for the individual's leaving? Have we created a situation in the work group that may cause others to leave, too? This, also, should come out of the interview.

Another reason for the interview is to check the organization's policies and working conditions. Are we matching the wrong people with the jobs? Are our hiring procedures creating bad situations? Are our policies out of date or out of line with other organizations? Is there something wrong with our wage structure? The answers to these questions may not be found in one interview, but clues may be seen in the things that are found out. So this is another reason for conducting exit interviews.

A final reason for these interviews is that they benefit the employees who are leaving. They may need to get some things off their chest. They may feel some remorse about leaving and the interview can help, as they talk about the decision they have made. Most important, they may be heading into some future trouble which can be prevented by a calm and rational talk. All of these become real, logical, and sound reasons for having the interview. But none of the results will be satisfactory if we do a poor job of conducting the interviews.

How do we conduct exit interviews? In the beginning, this type looks similar to the others, but there are some important differences. As usual, we want to put the interviewees at ease and let them know that we appreciate their taking the time to talk to us, even though they've made up their mind to leave us. We must immediately let them know that we feel they can help us and that we'd appreciate their help. And we want to assure them that we are not going to try to change anyone's mind about leaving. We want them to know that our every intention is to *listen*. We are looking for insight into our own problems and ways that we can improve the organization. Above all, we should put the interviewees at ease by letting them know we aren't going to pry or ask them to tell us all kinds of bad things about others in the group.

When an exit interview starts, *we start listening*. We ask open-ended questions designed to get the interviewees talking and *keep them talking*. We avoid interrupting them and do our best not to go on the defensive. We don't want it to get to be a "policy defense" interview. We correct any statements about policy that are obviously untrue but we don't have to defend them. No matter how much we'd like to launch into a statement about all the good things that these policies have accomplished, this isn't a time for us to be giving out information like that. We want to keep the disagreement to a minimum, so even when we correct a statement to supply the facts we do it by saying, "Well, it may have appeared that way, but actually the policy reads . . ." And when we come to a situation where there is no way to avoid disagreement, we need to say, "It's interesting that you feel that way," not "You're crazy if that's the way you think it is."

Exit interviews have one hazard that must be watched for and avoided. We must be sure not to let them degenerate into name-calling sessions about people in the group. Unless there is a substantial amount of evidence, there is no need to get into a discussion of specific people. Even in the face of this evidence, there is no reason to talk about people unless there's something useful to be gained by it. If there's someone in the office or some policy in the organization that is a well-known problem, this interview probably isn't the place to discuss it. Also, it makes more sense to talk only about those things that we can do something about. If interviewees want to talk about something that bothered them while they were working, but it is something that shouldn't have affected them, this, too, has no real place in the discussion.

## USE THE INFORMATION

In one respect, exit interviews are like all other interviews we have—we must learn to use the information we get. It's useless to take the time to gather information if we don't use it after we get it. Exit interviews may be the most important of all from this standpoint. Using the information from them may be the means of preventing other exit interviews in the future! We should study the information, and decide what we've really learned and how we can use it. If we have found a bad situation, we should correct it. If the information tells us that something we did caused a problem, we then take the necessary steps to see that it doesn't happen again. Finally, we should review our own actions during these interviews to see if we are satisfied with the way we conducted them. We ask ourselves:

"Did I plan it well?"

"Did I put the employee at ease?"

"Did it go as I planned it?"

"Did I really accomplish anything?"

"How did the employee feel when it was over?"

"How did I feel when it was over?"

"If I had it to do over again, would I do it differently?"

If the answer to this last question is "Yes," then we need to take whatever steps are necessary to see that we really do it differently the next time!

## FIRST CONCLUSION

Successful interviews don't just happen. They are carefully planned. It is an oversimplification to say that an interview is just a matter of two people talking to each other, but it's important to remember that that is basically just what it is. The purposes may be different from one interview to the next, the roles played by the interviewee and interviewer may change from one interview to the next, but still it comes down to our abilitiy to *talk with people.* There are times when we're trying to get information, as in an employment interview. Sometimes we want to give information, as in an appraisal interview. It may be that we just need to listen, mostly as we do in a counseling interview. But whatever kind we're involved in, we still are using the skills of talking with people on a one-to-one basis. We need to learn to plan the interview so we'll have a good idea of where we're going and when we've gotten there. We have to learn to ask questions properly, perhaps open-endedly or by using a reflective technique to keep the person talking. Perhaps we will have to be very direct and let the person know where he or she is missing the mark—and what the consequences are for not making the correction. These things aren't always easy to accomplish, and to be really good at them we have to practice, study our results, and practice some more. We have to be practicing the right thing, though, because practice only makes *permanent,* not necessarily *perfect.* If we practice the wrong thing long enough, we'll get good at being bad, and it will even begin to feel natural to us.

Listening is by far the hardest part of learning how to communicate. But in an interview, listening is most often the key to success. We can direct the interview by responding to whatever part of the interviewee's remarks we think will lead in the right direction, but this works only if we have been listening carefully to what is being said. Bad interviews result when we fail to take our turn at *listening.* This is more than just being quiet while the other person is talking. It's a matter of listening carefully, understanding, and responding properly. The steps in successful interviewing are simple enough to learn but take some concentration, mostly on setting our goals and then listening to see if we're getting the feedback that tells us we're going where we want to go. Once we've learned to be a good interviewer, it's surprising how much satisfaction we can get from conducting a successful interview. Since we're involved in so many interviews during our years as a supervisor, it behooves us to try for as much of this kind of satisfaction as we can get.

## THE CIVIL RIGHTS ACT AND THE EMPLOYMENT INTERVIEW

Title VII of the 1964 Civil Rights Act prohibits discrimination in employment on the basis of race, religion, color, national origin, or sex. A 1972 amendment to this act gives any minority person, or any woman, the right to enter a complaint against any business or other organization based on discrimination in hiring, promotion, pay, and related factors. In 1973 the Rehabilitation Act was passed making it unlawful to regard a person's handicap in consideration for jobs. The Equal Employment Opportunity Commission has the responsibility to administrate the equal-opportunity program. The passage of these Acts has led to many suits, charges, and judgments, which have resulted in the payment of millions of dollars in fines and adjustments. Also, many rulings that affect hiring and employment have been and still are being handed down. One area on which this has had the most telling effect has been the *employment interview.* Things that have traditionally been asked and discussed have been used as evidence in cases where discrimination has been charged. Even where intentions and motives were beyond question or things were done in innocence, rulings have gone against organizations because certain questions were asked which later could not be shown to have any direct bearing on the interviewee's ability to perform on the job. For these reasons, it is well worthwhile to go into detail about matters affecting the employment interview discussed earlier in this chapter.

### The problem

The job of the employment interviewer is to select people for the organization who will fit into the jobs that are available, and perhaps even move up in the organization's vertical structure. Historically, this has been a difficult job, because it places one in the position of being a prophet, a seer of the future, as well as part judge and part jury. Even at its best, employment interviewing has been something less than a science. Over the years, a series of questions was developed that would give interviewers a whole lot of information, with the idea that the greater the available information, the better the chances of successfully predicting a potential employee's use to an organization. There was a series of criteria which in themselves weren't intended to be biased, but when looked at in the light of equal employment hiring standards became very difficult to justify.

The most difficult thing was the absence of supporting data as to the relationship between the questions asked and the jobs to be done. There haven't been very good job descriptions; there haven't been very good job-skills descriptions; there has been an almost total lack of information supporting the relationship between hiring standards and job standards. Organizations had requirements of high school certificates, for example, but no information to show that the job required a high school diploma before the worker could perform satisfactorily. It wasn't a matter of whether or not it *was* a necessary thing, it just didn't have any proof behind it. It was eventually called into question because such a requirement often screened out minorities, and no one could show satisfactory data to *prove* that the requirement wasn't intended to be prejudicial.

There were other problems. Recruiters or employment interviewers were in the habit of giving tests to applicants. They would give standardized tests—which were valid in showing what was being tested for, but which had never been matched up against the performance of someone actually performing the job being filled. The testing had been regarded through the years as an acceptable way of screening people, with no thought of using it as a prejudicial tool against anyone, but the results were the same: it screened out many minorities, and no one could show that a certain test score was a guarantee of success at a certain job. In many cases, testing was discontinued as a screening device.

### No job standards

What was an even more serious problem, perhaps, was that the interviewers were never furnished an adequate breakdown of just what the jobs were that they were hiring people to fill. The job descriptions were almost always vague and full of generalities—often on purpose, for internal political reasons. In fact, in many if not most cases, the descriptions didn't even exist—on paper, at least. The only descriptions were those used in the case of union seniority cases, or where there was a reason to separate one job from another for promotion reasons. The job title might have been all that existed by way of description. There might be a title like "Staff Assistant" and another of a higher or lower grade like "Technical Assistant." Neither would be very clear, but one would be rated higher than the other, and if both were entrance jobs, one would have a higher cutoff score than another or perhaps require more education. When organizations were required to justify these things in light of the number of people who were screened out who were of minority status, it was impossible to do. Remember, for the most part, no bias was connected with the decisions to do it this way—it was just an expedient screening process that worked very well "mechanically."

What was really needed, of course, was a good, written description of the job to be filled, listing the kinds of skills that had been demonstrated as being required to do the job satisfactorily. This takes time, and requires knowledge both of the job and of how to write proper job descriptions. People with such knowledge often aren't available within the organization. Just as often, there is no one department that has been given this assignment or responsibility. In these cases, the job just didn't get done. What happened many times was that as pressure mounted, job descriptions got written—*after the fact.* As organizations saw that they were going to have trouble because they had turned down so many people who fit the minority status, they began to write descriptions. Such descriptions nearly always screened out the people *who had already been turned down.*

## A lack of communications

Another thing that compounded the problem was the fact that in large organizations, the recruiters or interviewers were far removed from the persons needing the employees hired. The employment office was far removed—in reporting if not in location—from the operating people, and rarely did they ever communicate very well with each other. The operations people would simply turn in a requirement for a certain number of people to fill certain jobs, and once this was approved by operations management and personnel, and was checked against the list of available people from other parts of the organization, the employment people took over. They probably did a very good job with the information they had, but they actually had very little. The end product was the hiring of people more or less blindly.

Later, when the question of discrimination came up, no one was able to explain just what it was the person hired was supposed to do. Since this was the case, neither was there anyone who could prove that the requirements set down for employment were really necessary for the job. In almost every case, somebody *felt* the requirements were just. Some said that, after all, we're really hiring for promotion later on. Some felt that it was their duty to hire the best person available. Some felt that they should continue to hire the "kind" of people who were already on the payroll, so that there would be a "compatibility" among the employees. Then, too, there were some who were just plain prejudiced against certain people because of their race or creed or sex or place of national origin. Since the law—like society—is unable to determine which people are actually prejudiced and which aren't, it was much easier to deal with the acts of discrimination than to try to decide on people's biases. Hence the law stepped in and ruled against the various forms of discrimination. Later, of course, the law was expanded to forbid any discrimination against handicapped people. There were those who predicted that all this would bring doom to the hiring place. But doom just never did arrive. We'll see now how organizations have dealt with the law and what the law allows. It is not our purpose to show how to beat the law, but to show how to live within the law and still get the best employees available under the restrictions and limitations of the various laws. We'll deal primarily with the employment interview, since that's where most of the violations—and the resulting suits and fines—occur.

## The employment interview itself

It is a far easier job to state what we're *not* allowed to ask than to clearly state what *is* permitted. In many cases the jury is still out as far as clarity is concerned. Cases are pending, trials are in appeals courts, and investigations are under way to see if the laws have been violated. What is allowed one day might be disallowed the next. It sounds more confusing than it actually is, however. There are some rules of thumb that can keep most questions and questioners within the law and avoid discrimination.

The single most important thing to remember is that no question should be asked without good reason; there must be a direct relationship between the questions asked and the job to be filled. And the same question may be legitimate in one case and completely out of order in another. For instance, if the job requires that the employee use his or her own car, it certainly is necessary to ask, "Do you own your own car?" If it does not, then that question is not permissible. Likewise, if a job requires typing, then we obviously must ask the interviewee whether he or she can type. But if it does not, then we just as obviously must not ask that question.

## Planning the interview

How can we avoid asking the wrong questions—or make sure that we do ask the right questions? Simply by doing a good job of planning. First, we never hire anybody without knowing the job they will be required to fill. Second, we make sure we have enough information about the job to do a good interview for it. We analyze the job until we're able to list all the duties and responsibilities of the person who fills it. We compare responsibilities and duties of the job with the qualifications of the person who has applied for it, and make sure that we're looking only at the minimum requirements. If these include some personal abilities or characteristics, such as meeting people or answering the phone, then we make note of this, too. We look at people we've hired previously and see if we've hired below this qualification level before.

The next job of planning is for the interview itself. We decide on the type of questions we'll ask to get the kind of information we want. As much as possible, we even rehearse some of these questions to see how they sound to us, and to make ourselves comfortable with them before we ask them of the applicant. We study the applicant's forms before the interview. We mark those things we want *and need* more information on, and we list other things that aren't dealt with on the application but that we want *and need* to know. As far as possible, we make a general outline covering the flow of questioning as we would like to see it go. (We can even reveal this to the applicant if we wish, so he or she will be able to understand just where we're headed with each question.) From here on, it's a matter of preparing for a normal good interview with regard to its key elements: place—comfortable and private; time—adequate, undisturbed; materials—available and familiar.

### What we can—and can't—ask

From here on, we'll talk about some of the things that can and can't be asked, bearing in mind that we've established the groundwork for determining the kind of information we need.

It is legal to ask for date of birth and proof of that age—
but illegal to show preference for younger persons in hiring.

It is legal to ask if the person can meet the work schedule and attendance requirements—
but illegal to ask specifics about the person's spouse, the spouse's employment, or who will look after the children.

It is legal to ask about the training and experience the person had in the military of the United States—
but illegal to ask about reasons for discharge, or about service in the military of other governments, or for copies of discharge papers.

It is legal to ask about how long the applicant plans to stay on the job or about any expected absences, providing the questions are asked of both men and women—
> but illegal to ask direct questions about pregnancies or about previous pregnancies.

It is legal to ask for names the person has used with this organization or with other organizations for reference purposes—
> but illegal to ask about the origin of a name or anything about a name that would reveal its owner's marital status.

It is legal to ask a person's height or size, *if* it has been shown that such height or size is a requirement for the job and that no one can or has done it without meeting the stated requirements—
> but illegal to ask about height or size if there is no job requirement relating to these things.

It is legal to ask if the person can be cleared for work lawfully in this country and can provide such proofs *after hiring*—
> but illegal to ask for proof of citizenship or in what country the person is a citizen.

It is legal to ask that a photograph be supplied for record purposes *after* employment—
> but illegal to ask for a photograph *before* hiring.

It is legal to ask for an address where the person can be contacted—
> but illegal to ask with whom the person is living or whether the person owns or rents his or her home.

*It is always illegal to ask questions regarding marital status, race, color, religion, creed, or sex.*

## SECOND CONCLUSION

In conclusion to our discussion of Civil Rights and the employment interview, we can only add that employers are hiring and rejecting people every day without violating any laws or discriminating against anyone in the process. Good employees are being hired, too, and jobs are being filled with qualified people. Until we learned how to understand the law, and how to determine just what the job really required in the way of skills, things were pretty rough. Many unqualified people were probably hired just because the interviewer was afraid to turn them down and bring on a suit or investigation. These days are rapidly passing as we get smarter and know more about how to conduct the employment interview. Above all, we want to get the best person for the job and have no interest in discriminating against anyone. To make certain this is what happens in our interviewing, we need to study the things mentioned here and be sure to check with our own organization and its policies on hiring and interviewing. If there is a fault with this section, it may be that it is oversimplified. For that reason, we urge you not to depend entirely on what is here, but to continue seeking additional information and advice from within your own organization.

## EXERCISES

1. Group multiple role play: Have the group divide into subgroups of three each. One is to be the interviewer, one the interviewee, and the other the observer. Those being interviewed are to play themselves. Each is being considered for a completely different assignment. The idea is to find out each person's viewpoint toward a change of jobs within the organization which will necessitate relocating to another town. The organization will pay the moving expenses and care for the sale of real estate, but there is no pay increase. There is opportunity for advancement in a couple of years, and while no promises can be made, the chances are pretty good that a promotion will result if the employee doesn't mess up on the new job. The observer should look for the steps in successful interviewing, such as: putting the employee at ease; stating the purpose of the interview; asking open and reflective questions; dealing with questions; summarizing action to be taken as a result of the interview; and concluding the interview on good terms.

2. Group multiple role play: When the above role plays are completed, have the participants rotate positions, with the observer now being interviewed and the interviewee becoming the interviewer. The former interviewer becomes the observer. When this is over, have the people report their successes and failures. Record the things that were difficult to do, and areas where they need to improve.

3. Subgroup exercise: In small groups discuss why disciplinary interviews are dreaded and what we might do to overcome this feeling. Decide whether there is a justification for the dread and see whether anyone has had a bad experience with an employee they've had to discipline. Bring the group back together and see what they've

found out. Make a list of the most often used excuses for not doing disciplinary interviews and decide how many of these are justified.

4. Individual exercise: Ask the participants to think about themselves as they were when they started with their present organization. Think of what questions were asked and list them down the left side of a piece of paper. On the right side of the sheet put a checkmark by those things that were really important to the job the person actually had. When all have finished, collect the typical questions and record on the board. Save for further use.

5. Group activity: Look at the items from exercise 4 and decide what question we really need to ask a person we're considering hiring. See if there are any questions that get into the interview through custom or tradition. See if we can eliminate any of them just because they don't relate to the job to be done. This isn't easy and shouldn't be taken as an excuse for not asking anything! We do need much information and this is the time to get it, before the employee comes to work with us.

6. Group activity: Examine the questions collected from exercise 4 and see how many of them might be construed as discriminatory if the person hadn't been hired. In other words, which of these questions could have been used against an organization if a person wanted to bring a charge of some kind against it for violating the EEOC requirements?

# 10
# TRAINING: THE SUPERVISOR'S RESPONSIBILITY

One of the biggest mistakes supervisors—new and old—make is to assume that training is an adjunct to their regular job, something they do only when they have plenty of time and nothing else to do. A supervisor who has this attitude really doesn't understand his or her job very well, since the real function of the supervisor is to get work done through other people. Taking this another step, we can say that our *prime* job is to see that our people are trained. If we have anyone under us who can't do their job because they haven't been trained, then we have fallen down on the job as far as that person is concerned. Unless our people are properly trained, we have no real justification for appraising them, or for finding fault with their work. Training, then, becomes an important part of our job, and we will do well to learn how to train others if we expect to succeed as supervisors.

## TRAINING IS A SKILL

Unfortunately, there are many people around who want to classify the ability to train others as an art or a science. Maybe it is, but it is a skill first, and like any other skill it must be learned. Sometimes we go in the opposite direction—we tend to think of training others as something we can do without any special skill. After all, we say, what's so hard about telling someone how to do something we know all about? The problem is, that's what we usually do and call it training—we "tell" someone how to do it, and *telling isn't training.*

There are many skills supervisors have to learn. We must learn to write, speak, conduct interviews, and train our people. Unfortunately, we can do these things in such a way that it will *look* like we're doing all right when we actually aren't. We watch people doing some training and it looks and sounds like they're doing a good job, but we may be fooled by what we see and hear. The people being trained may not really get the message and may go away frustrated. The people doing the training may think they have done well, and go about their business thinking the employees should do their jobs satisfactorily. Later we may hear the trainers say, "Don't you remember, I told you last week how to do that?" The point is that *the employees get the blame for the poor job of training done by the supervisors.* So we must learn how to train; that is, we must learn the skill of training others.

There are some things we can put off learning, but training must be learned very quickly if we are to get the most work out of our people. Not only must we learn how to train others quickly, but we must learn how to do it *well.* Every time we do a poor job of training someone, we waste time that can't be recovered, and we also get ourselves into the dilemma of not knowing whether to train over again or let the employee go on doing the job only half well. The truth is, we rarely repeat the training, but we do end up spending a lot of time trying to repair damage done by poorly trained employees. The worst thing that can happen, of course, is that we end up blaming the employees for not being able to do their jobs when we've really failed at ours.

But we can learn the basic skill of training others, if we recognize it as a skill and work hard at learning it. We cannot assume that, just because we know the job we're training the employees to do, we also know how to train someone on that job. Operating a drill press or

changing the ribbon on a typewriter is quite different from *training* someone on how to operate the press or change the ribbon. There are steps to training that we can identify and measure. We can tell whether or not we have done a good job and we can improve on the skill once we learn what it is that makes up the skill. Let's take a look at the skill in more detail and see just what it is that makes up this thing that some want to take for granted.

## WHY TRAIN?

If we ask whether training is necessary, the obvious answer is, "Of course." But if we ask why we train, we get some strange answers. Some train just because there is money in the budget. Others train because the employees expect it. There are those who train because higher management has decreed that it be done. Others train only when they have spare time, then they train to fill up the time. None of these are reasons for training. Basically, there are only three good reasons for training.

1. The employee can't do the job.
2. The employee can do it but not well enough.
3. The employee is doing the job incorrectly.

In the first case—not being able to do the job—it may be that the employees are new and have never done it before. This is an obvious case for training, but there are those who say, "Experience is the best teacher—let them learn the hard way like I did." This isn't a very practical approach from the standpoint of efficiency. Maybe the employees will be better able to do the job after they have made numerous mistakes, but who pays for all those mistakes? Who "unlearns" the employees of all the things they'll have learned to do incorrectly? If the employees are new, then for their benefit and that of the organization, it's our job to see that they have an opportunity to start off learning the right way to do their jobs. Only then can we get an accurate picture of how well they're performing and progressing. But it may be that the job is new, never having been performed before by anyone in the organization. It may be a new procedure or a new piece of equipment. Here, again, the employees have a right to get started on the right foot. Also, for the good of the new policy, let's get the job done correctly from the beginning. Anytime we introduce something new there will be enough problems without us complicating things by doing a poor job of training.

The second case—training because the employees can't do the job well enough—isn't quite as simple as the first case. It may be that the employees haven't been trained and have picked up some of the job on their own. We need to speed up their production and save on wasted time. Now we are faced with the question of whether or not to train, because after all, the employees know something about the job already. We have to weigh the time and expense of training against the advantages of doing the job faster or better. The same is true even if the employees actually had some training at one time, but need more in order to meet the standards set for our organization. We have to decide how much it's worth to get the improvement we can get from training.

Finally, there are the employees who are actually doing the job incorrectly. This is valid ground for training. How do we know the employees aren't able to do the job? We may be able to tell just by the number of errors that can be traced directly to them. It may be that a survey of some kind has caused us to look more closely at each employee and we see that some are failing to do their jobs correctly. It may even be that watching the employees work convinces us quickly that they actually don't know what they're doing. This sounds like reason enough for training, but we need to ask ourselves one basic question before we do any training: "If the employees' lives depended on it, could they do the job correctly?" If the answer to this is "Yes," then training isn't the answer; there is some other problem and training won't solve it. So when we train, we must be sure to ask ourselves which is the reason we are training: to enable the employees to do the job; to enable them to do it better; or to enable them to do it correctly. We need to ask this question for *each* employee we train.

This all sounds simpler than it really is. If we aren't careful, we'll find ourselves training someone who has had the training some time ago. To compound the problem, the employee's performance may even go up for some time right after the training, especially if he or she enjoys getting away from the job for awhile. But the chances are good that the employee will just do poorly in the training session and go back to the job wondering what kind of a supervisor we are to provide training he or she has already had. Even worse, we end up giving training a bad name; because the employee can't do the job any better after the training, some will conclude that training is a waste of time.

Another possibility for error is to train someone who isn't really going to have time to apply what he or she is learning, Maybe the employee is just a few months away from retiring or moving to another job. Everyone else in the section has had the training so we schedule him or her for it, also. It's fine to worry about our employee's feelings, but if we send this employee because we don't want to hurt anyone's feelings, we need to remember that it's also good to worry about the organization's money. How can we justify spending training money when it's obvious we can't get our money back from an employee who just won't be on the job that long?

There is another time when it is a mistake to train: when we train an employee we want to see promoted. We don't train because he or she needs it or can do a better job for us, but because it will look good on his or her record to have had this particular training program. Unless this is a part of the employee's regular development program, we've made a mistake in training for this reason. The problem may come back to us in a strange way; it may get around that we have set a precedent that anyone who takes this kind of training expects to be promoted, or everyone wants to be sent to the training program because they think it's the way to move up. In either case, we've put an undue burden on the training program and asked it to do something it wasn't intended to do.

Finally, one other thing that helps get us into trouble is to train someone we know hasn't got a chance to learn the job because of his or her background or lack of experience. Some supervisors send certain people to training programs to prove a point—that the employee is incompetent. Again, we've used training in the wrong way, and have failed to properly do our job—which is to train the right people for the right reasons.

## PREPARING TO TRAIN

Before we can do any training of our own, we must determine just what it is we want to train our employees to do. This sounds simple enough, but it really isn't. For example, we should be sure we know exactly what standard of performance we are looking for. This means analyzing the job to make sure we can train someone else to perform according to the organization standard—that is, to do the right thing in the right time with no more than the acceptable number of errors. The standard isn't what someone else has done on that same job that we thought was pretty good. It's not what has come to be accepted as the average for employees doing this particular job. It's what the organization has set as a standard for the *job itself*. We need to learn to set job standards by

looking at the work, not the employees who are now or have been doing the job.

Before we train, we'd better get policy questions settled, too. We'd
better find out if there are changes in the mill that will make our standards wrong. If there are acceptable deviations from the job standard,
we'd better know about them before we start to train. There's no reason
to be afraid to ask questions about standards, because we can never be
sure that our training has really been done properly if we don't know
what the standard actually is. Remember, many so-called standards exist
only because everyone has just accepted them without question—maybe
even perpetuating error or mediocrity in the process. This is particularly
true with things like work flow. Just because filing cabinets got placed
in a certain place at one time, work may flow unevenly around them,
even though it would be much more efficient to move them closer to
the work operation. As a result of this poor arrangement, the work has
suffered, but the "standard" has been set. If we don't watch out,
we'll find ourselves training to this standard. We find this to be true
with such things as forms and sales slips, too. We try to train someone
to fill out a complicated form or slip without ever questioning just why
the form is so complex. The truth may be that it got that way because
every once in a while someone added something to it without trying to
cut out anything. Pretty soon it got unwieldy but we keep on using it
as the standard and trying to train people to use it. A few well-chosen
questions might help "uncomplicate" the forms. In fact, just listening
to our employees might be some help. They probably know that some
things are unnecessary but no one has ever bothered to ask them. Remember, they are doing the job, so no one else can be more familiar
with what is actually being done than they are. If we can't come up
with a better reason for doing something or not doing it a certain way,
we should take their word for it.

It's highly unlikely that we can ever train on everything that needs
attention, so we have to decide early in the game just what it is we are
going to include in the training program for each of the employees. For
example, for new employees, we should concentrate on those things
that will be likely to come up first in their new assignments. They'll
have enough to do to learn the things they'll be doing immediately
without worrying about things that will come up several months from
now. If the job is being changed, we should concentrate on the changes,
not the entire job. It's wasteful (and boring to the employees) to go
through operations that the employees already understand. Even after

we have decided what to do our training on, we should still check and see if there are any existing programs that will do the job for us. Maybe the organization already has some kind of program that will come close enough to doing our job for us so that it wouldn't be worthwhile for us to develop an entire training program to make up the difference. It's always well to check this out before going too far. By the way, we mustn't forget to check with other departments about their training programs. Sometimes we get so out of touch with others in the same organization that we don't even know that they have the same training problems that we have and may be conducting programs very similar to the ones we are preparing. We ask oursleves, "Why hasn't someone done this kind of training before?" Then we ask, "Who else has the same kind of training problems I do?" The answers to these questions should help us screen the market well enough to prevent us from inventing the wheel all over again.

Once we've decided on what training needs to be done and why we're doing it, we must set some realistic objectives or goals for the training we are going to do. The simplest way to do this is to ask, "What is it I want them to be able to do when the training is over?" Basically, the answer to this question depends on the answers to the following ones:

What actions do I want from them?

What standards do I plan to use to gauge their success?

What limitations or tolerances can I live with?

If we've taken a good look at the job as we suggested earlier, these things should be clear by now. We should know what a satisfactory job is, and if we don't, it will show up when we attempt to answer these questions. It's not enough to just say, "We want them to understand how the framus machine works." We have to specify the action and the degree of tolerance we expect to allow. Requiring that the operator produce 100 items an hour with no more than two errors is much more specific than requiring that he or she understand how to use the machine. One reason training is so haphazard is that we go about it in a haphazard manner. We just suddenly discover ourselves doing some training without much real planning. When we do a sloppy job of planning, we do a sloppy job of training. The planning doesn't have to be elaborate or time-consuming. A plan can be written out on the back of an envelope, *but it should be done.* We need to decide where the training is going to take place, just who will be trained, and when it will be done.

## DO IT RIGHT

It seems ridiculous to say it, but when we train, we should do a good job of it. As silly as it sounds, though, we find that some training is better than other training, hence some people are doing a better job than others. The reason is that we don't always know a good training job when we see one. Supervisors can be heard to say, "Don't you remember, I *told* you . . . ," which means that they think "telling" and "training" are the same thing. In fact, when we watch them "train," they end up doing most of the talking and the showing, then leave with a statement like, "Any questions?" The employees think they understand; the operation looked simple enough, but after the supervisor leaves, the employees find that they can't really do the job after all. They feel pretty stupid because they've just seen the supervisor do it and heard an explanation and didn't have any questions—all because *the supervisor did a poor job of training.* Since training is a skill, we can't expect to be good at it right away. We can try to learn the skill, though, and as we do more and more of it we can evaluate the results and grow with it.

Good training follows specific steps and procedures. When we train people on the job, what *we do* will have a definite bearing on how well they can perform in the future. The most accepted process to use is a simple, three-step one that has worked well for many years. It goes like this:

STEP 1

We tell them what to do.

We do it correctly.

STEP 2

They tell us what to do.

We do it correctly.

STEP 3

They tell us what to do.

They do it correctly.

Note the purpose of each step. In Step 1, we tell the employees what is to be done so there will be no doubt about the action and so they will be mentally involved. Then we do it correctly, being sure they see each part of the procedure. Then in Step 2, they are still involved mentally as they tell us what to do, and if they tell us correctly, we do it correctly again. In Step 3, they tell us what they're going to do, but do not do it until we have agreed that they're right. If they are, then we let them do it. Step 3 can be repeated several times for practice, but it's always a good idea to keep the employees involved mentally as much as possible. After all, this is where the memory is established. Even though we want the employees to develop good work habits, we still want them to perform from a good mental attitude. To increase this mental involvement, we can expand the three-step process to include not only *what,* but *why* and *how.* We still go through each step as described above, but after going through *what,* we repeat the process by telling *how.* Then we repeat with *why* we perform the operation the way we are doing it. In other words, the first time through we simply worry about the employees seeing, hearing, and doing the right thing. They see how, but we don't go into it in much detail. Then we repeat the process, this time adding a description of *how* we do it—so that the employees hear a description of the correct way to perform the operation, while doing it. Finally, we go over the *what* and *how,* but add to it the reasons *why* we use a certain movement or tie it a certain way, or move the ribbon to the left.

It should be obvious that when we are doing this kind of training, we have the employees use the actual equipment, or something that looks just like what they will be using. Ideally, they should be trained on the equipment they use every day, right at the spot where they do the job. If not, then we should try to find idle equipment that is like the kind they'll be using. As a final alternative, we can use something that closely simulates the regular thing they use, but we should remember that the less imagination they have to use, the better they will be trained. If they get dirty on the job, they should get dirty during the training. If they write on blue paper on the job, they should have blue paper during the training. By the way, there's a simple point that we miss a lot of the time: When we train, we never *face* the employees; we always show them from the same position they will take when they do the work. If we face them, they will see everything done backwards and may become quite confused when they try doing it themselves.

## CLASSROOM TRAINING

Occasionally, supervisors will be asked to conduct some form of classroom training. It may be that they have become expert in certain fields or that they have been selected to study a particular subject and teach in an organizational school of some kind. Occasionally, supervisors have enough people working under them so that they find it easier to do the training all at one time in some kind of classroom setting. For that reason, we will talk a little bit about how to do this kind of training most effectively. There is more to teaching a group than just having a knowledge of the subject and more to it than just being able to make a good speech. The idea is to change some people's behavior on the job, which is the same reason for doing on-the-job training. Up to this point, everything we've said about preparing for on-the-job training pretty well holds true for classroom training. We have to know what it is we want the people to be able to do; there needs to be a standard, and it helps if we know the deficiencies of the people in the classroom. Once we've done all this and found out what we need to know about the standards and the performance deficiencies of the employees, we're ready to go into the classroom. Let's see what we need to know to make this effort top notch.

There are some basic rules for classroom training that will help us understand our job better. First, people learn more by participating in the learning activity than they do by being told what they need to know. We can tell them much faster if they aren't involved in saying things or doing things, but they can forget just as fast! Next, we should realize that the students are more likely to remember those things they figure out for themselves than those we figure out for them. This means that we need to let them "discover" some of the information for themselves, especially the conclusions. In some circles this technique is called *discovery learning.* That's a good name for it, because that's exactly what happens: The instructor gives the class members enough information to enable them to figure out the rest on their own. The instructor leads them along with new information, building on what they already know, then stops with a question aimed at making them think about where all of this is leading. At this point, if we've done the job right, they'll get a big "Aha!" reaction and we'll have caused them to discover what it was we wanted them to learn. As a result, they'll remember it longer.

The next thing to keep in mind is that they will be more likely to remember and learn those things that relate most to their jobs. If they are given some information or shown some kind of new operation with the knowledge that they will be expected to use it when they get back on the job, they'll be much more likely to work at learning it than if they hear, "Some day you may need this, so you'd better pay attention." The good instructor will build in examples of application of these things, and have a good storehouse of incidents in which there is use of the new material back on the job.

Obviously, not all students have the same background, not all have the same interest in learning, and not all of them have the same ability to grasp all the subjects. This brings up another thing to remember: If they aren't all learning the same way, *we may have to teach in different ways to reach different ones.* For some, a lecture may be fine because they've always been able to grasp quickly from a lecture. For others, repeating may be important, because it takes awhile for the material to soak in. Still others may require some discussion or different examples or different approaches. All of these things have to be mixed into each teaching session because we can't always tell which students are learning best in which way.

This leads us to the next point to remember in making ourselves good instructors. We'll know what's being learned by whom only when *we hear them tell us or see them showing us.* In teaching jargon, this is called "getting feedback." Just as we talked about the importance of it in Chapter 5, on communications, and for the same reasons, it's extremely important here in our teaching efforts. If we pay attention only to what *we're saying,* we won't know what the students are learning. If we get feedback from only one or two, we'll have a general idea of how well we're doing, but we won't know for sure how the class is doing until we hear all of them saying things and reacting to what we've been teaching. When we mention feedback, the idea of testing comes to mind. This isn't what we're talking about here. For example, simply by having the class break into small groups and come up with an agreement on a certain question, it will take only a matter of a few minutes to find out how well we've gotten our point across. If there is much discussion and little agreement, we'd better start over or review. If they quickly come up with a common answer, we can reinforce this and go on.

While we're talking about differences in the classroom, we should point out that one very good way of overcoming differences as a problem is to have the less experienced ones work with the more experiencd ones, or the less interested or slower learners work with those who are more interested or quicker. This puts some of the responsibility on the better students and they will actually learn more as they try to help one another along. Most of the time, students learn from one of their classmates as well as or better than they do from one of the instructors.

We said that good teaching is more than good public speaking. Let's make sure we understand that *bad* public speaking, that is, mumbling, distracting mannerisms, poor use of the visual aids equipment, etc., has to be overcome by even better teaching techniques. We can ruin some very good instructional efforts by poor speaking efforts. Not that our students will necessarily get much more from the speaking itself if it's polished and "stageworthy," but at least we won't detract from the learning effort if we make a good try at speaking well!

## FOLLOW UP ON TRAINING

One final word about training: We shouldn't just train and go off and leave it. We should follow up on what we have done and see how well the training "took." Training is more than doing it, marking the training record, then forgetting about it and the employees, and saying "Well, that job is complete." We should go back to the employees and see how they're doing. Check their performance against the standard we set. Check error rates, look at outputs, see if the secretary's letters are better—whatever the training was on. If the employees are performing well, we can take credit for a job well done. If not, then we need to take a look at our procedures to see if we failed to do the job properly. The rule in this case is simple: If the employees are doing something we trained them on, *we are responsible for their performance until we find out that something other than their training is keeping them from doing the job.* Of course, we are always responsible for their performance in a way, but now we look for some other cause because we are satisfied that the training has been done correctly. If we follow the proper procedures, we can be sure that the training *has* been done correctly.

## CONCLUSION

Training is the supervisor's responsibility. That's the heading of this chapter. It's the message within it. It's the conclusion we need to reach when we study about training. Training subordinates to reach their potential is a serious thing, and one that can have serious consequences if not done correctly. The dangerous thing about poor training is that often it isn't the supervisor but the poorly trained employees themselves who get the blame. Although their records show that they were trained, their performance is suffering, and they will be shown as below-standard performers on those records. To make it worse, the employees may think they've been trained and give themselves a bad rating in their own minds, perhaps believing they just aren't capable of learning. To try to emphasize this need to do a good job of training, let's think of it in this way:

It's now appraisal time. Our employees are going to be evaluated on how well they've done in their jobs over a certain period of time. Hopefully there is a standard that is understood by both them and us as to how well they should be doing those jobs. We have no right to appraise them, however, if we've failed to properly train them up to that standard. Suppose we've not trained them as well as we should have. We've put in some training time, but not very skillfully, though the training time is entered on their records. Because the employees have not had the right training, they aren't doing their jobs up to standard. In the appraisal, we make an entry to this effect. How honest and fair is that? Shouldn't we rather make an entry that says, "Due to poor training, this employee has not yet been able to perform up to standard?" Of course, we aren't likely to make such an entry, but the employee will suffer from the poor appraisal for a long time to come. It may even be a permanent part of his or her record, and all because we didn't do our job well. On the other hand, think about it from the standpoint of having done a good job. It's now appraisal time and our employees are doing their jobs up to standard. Even though we aren't likely to say that they are doing well because we did such a good job of training, we can take the satisfaction of knowing that when we did our job properly our employees responded with good performances, and that, too, will be on their records for a long time. We can be pleased with this kind of result, especially if we get it often. And we will, if we learn our training skills well!

## EXERCISES

1. Two-group exercise: Divide the group into two sections. Have one section take the position that training is a skill that has to be learned, can be measured, and can be done poorly or well or in between. Let them develop their arguments in favor of this in small subgroups within their section. One person should serve as their spokesperson. The other half of the group should operate the same way, in small subgroups and with a spokesperson for the entire half-group. Their position is that good training is an art that comes from being gifted as an instructor. Some few things can be learned, but for the most part a person either is a good instructor or is not, and trying to develop the skill will not aid appreciably. When the subgroups have finished their activity and combined their findings within their own sections, each section's spokesperson should be briefed for a discussion as outlined in exercise 2 below.

2. Group exercise: The two sections should debate their sides now and a list of their points should be recorded on the board. All group members should be urged to take notes from each section's discussion. When the two sections have exhausted their discussion, the group as a whole should take a look at the points made and determine how valid they are. "Sides" should no longer be considered at this point; rather, everyone should begin to look at the points made with an eye to seeing how to best learn the *skill of teaching.*

3. Small-group activity: Divide the whole group into several small subgroups, each of which should pick a job that is common to all of its members, or at least familiar enough so that each member can contribute something in the discussion and exercise. The job should be a simple one, even a part of a job. Each subgroup should analyze the job they have selected a piece at a time, until they have it broken down into individual operations. When they have it thus broken down, they should set a standard for each of the operations. The standard should tell not only *how* the job is to be done, but *how well* or *how often in a period of time,* etc. In other words, the standard should be *measurable* and *observable.* When the subgroups have gotten this information, they should be ready to present it to the entire group, having picked a spokesperson to represent them.

4. Group activity: Using the information on standards from exercise 3, let each spokesperson present his or her findings, with the rest of the subgroup doing the "defending." The idea is for the whole group to see that we often try to train on things for which we haven't set a standard, hence shouldn't expect to do too good a job of training. (If we don't know how well we want the employee to perform, how can we know how well we've trained him or her?)

# 11

# HOW TO RUN A GOOD MEETING (CONFERENCE LEADERSHIP)

Much has been said—very little of it complimentary—about all of the meetings that are usually run in an organization. Committees meet, groups meet, managers meet, supervisors meet—and meet some more. There is little chance that we will change this, nor do we really want to. Meetings are a way of life and, to a large extent, the thread of life in most organizations. The reason we make fun of them or complain about them is they take up a lot of our time—often seeming to waste it—and usually come at a time when we just don't have a moment to spare. It may just be, however, that one of the main reasons we feel as we do about meetings is that we've never experienced the satisfaction of attending and being part of a well-run meeting, one that accomplished specific goals, did it quickly and efficiently, and terminated when the purpose had been met. It's to that end that this chapter is dedicated. We are going to try to establish the basis for conducting meetings that do just these things.

## PREPARING FOR THE CONFERENCE

As we have said, conferences (meetings) are a way of life in the organization. Without proper control they can run poorly and accomplish very little. Run properly, they can accomplish things that cannot be done in any other way. The first thing we need to accept is that meetings have a precise purpose. They are necessary, hence we should approach them with a positive attitude. We should also approach them with an idea of knowing what the particular purpose of any specific meeting is. Is it a *problem-solving* session? Have problems arisen that we need to attack in a group? If so, then we must approach the meeting with the information needed for problem-solving. We need to set it up so we can go through the steps in problem-solving. Is the purpose of the meeting *decision-making*? If so, we will need to remember that no one should leave the meeting without knowing exactly what final decision was reached. We will need to remember that someone must be responsible for carrying out that decision. In other words, we will need to aim everything about the conference at decision-making. We will need to use good decision-making techniques in the meeting. Since we are leading the meeting, we are responsible for seeing that these techniques are followed.

Is the purpose of the meeting *brainstorming*? Has someone decided that the best way to reach a solution or develop an idea or attack a problem is to have a group of people get together and do some brainstorming? If so, then we must be sure that all of the conditions of brainstorming are met and that we understand the process. Will we have the necessary supplies for recording the ideas? Will we have ourselves conditioned to avoid letting any negative thinking get into the session? Again, since we are conducting the meeting, it is our responsibility to see that everything goes well. But we need to establish the purpose in our minds so we can make the necessary arrangements.

Perhaps the purpose is *attitude development.* It may be that the meeting is to be no more than a "pep rally," aimed at increasing loyalty or improving sales. Maybe there is a quality-control problem and this meeting is for the purpose of changing attitudes toward this matter. If so, we need to know it, and to aim in that direction. Even if the meeting is just for the purpose of educating our group on new policy or product or services, or about a new benefit plan, we should settle this in our minds and build our planning around it.

The point is that if we are going to run the meeting, we need to know its specific purpose. After all, we're asking a number of people to give up work time and come to the meeting. They have a right to expect that we are going to know what the real objective of the conference is and what they are trying to accomplish. As conference leaders, then, we ask ourselves, "What *specific activities* will take place?" This is important in the arrangement of furniture, the getting of equipment, the selection of rooms, etc. The activities will determine whether we will need to seat everyone in a circle, provide tables, or maybe just set up chairs facing the front. Thinking of these things ahead of time will make us look good and certainly help make the meeting a success. But we need to know more. We should decide on the *specific timing* for the meeting—not just how long it will run, but when we will have it. What

day? What time of day? If it's to be a one-hour meeting, why run it at a time that would conflict with an already established coffee break? On the other hand, if it's to be a lengthy one, providing for a break in the middle might be a good way to inject some relief. Having meetings at the end of the day (or week), when everyone is tired and thinking about going home, might not be the best time to get into a brainstorming session. If we aren't sure how long the meeting will take, running it too close to lunch or quitting time may get us into trouble. Suppose it turns out we need more time! What often happens here is that when time starts to run out, and we don't want to have to call another meeting, we begin to make hurried decisions or leave some things hanging loose. When the meeting is over and we review our accomplishments, we discover that some important things got overlooked, or that some of the things we decided aren't really very practical after all. Finally, on specifics, the conference leader needs to know the *specific attendance.* Not just how many are going to attend, but *who.* There is always the consideration of seating, both as to who sits where and how many seats will be required. If the leader has any control over the selection of those who attend, he or she needs to go back and look at the meeting's specific objective. If this is to be an education meeting, then maybe the more people in attendance the better. On the other hand, if there is to be problem-solving or decision-making, the number needs to be held to a minimum. The basic requirement for the latter kind of meeting is to have enough there to represent everybody concerned, but not to weight it with too many people from one side of the argument or from one department. Conferees don't like to be put in the position of having the meeting stacked against them in numbers. They have just as much right to their opinion as others, but if the "other side" brought along more than their share of representatives, then things are unequal. The conferees will know this in a hurry, too. The way to avoid this is to look at the list of suggested attendees and decide whether there is fair representation from all departments, groups, factions, etc. If not, a telephone call or private suggestion may be the best way to solve the problem. As we have said, these things make a lot of difference in the outcome of conferences, and conference leaders should do whatever they can to control the attendance, and the particular people attending.

## PHYSICAL FACILITIES

Of all the things that can make or break a meeting, perhaps nothing can have more influence than the place where the meeting is held and the equipment used in the meeting. No matter how well the leader coordinates the timing and the speaking and the interchange of ideas and movement of information, if the room is poorly ventilated, or too hot or too cold, all of this will go to accomplish very little. Actually, setting up the facilities isn't difficult when we consider some basic elements. We can divide the problem areas as follows:

Creature comforts

Acoustics

Visibility

Interference

Let's look at them individually. First, the creature comforts—those things that affect our senses, starting with the ventilation we have already mentioned. Is the air being changed frequently enough by the ventilating system? Is there a means of regulating the temperature *in a hurry* if the room gets too hot or too cold? We want to be sure to have control of the facility, by the way, as far as the temperature is concerned. If someone in another room can regulate the temperature in our room, we've obviously got a problem. The same is true if the system is centrally controlled. If the only control we have is to open and close doors and windows, we might want to consider whatever other facilities are available. Many other things affect our comfort, some of which are a little subtle. For example, we can sit in a molded plastic chair and it will feel very comfortable. But after a short time it becomes very uncomfortable, because it was molded for one position—and the trouble with that is that we don't sit in one position very long. As soon as we change from the position the chair was molded for, we're in a chair that won't fit us. Many people find it difficult to remain comfortable very long in chairs that don't have arms. As long as there is a table to lean on it's not too bad, but when they try to lean back or relax, their arms drop to their sides in a strained way. Which brings up another problem that's easy to overlook: the height of the table above the chair. If the table is too high or too low, again the conferees find themselves straining to get comfortable. We need to remember that these aren't things that we can tell just by sitting down for a few moments. If we want to try out the furniture, we must try several positions—sitting with our arms on the table, then at our sides, leaning back in the chair, sitting in one position for a few minutes. How does all of this feel? Remember, too, that there is such a thing as being *over-comfortable*. If the meeting is likely to produce a few periods of boredom, soft easy chairs won't add to the alertness of the group.

The matter of acoustics is obviously of importance, but there are some problems that may not be apparent from just looking at a facility. For example, sound carries better in an empty room than in a full one. Even if the room appears to carry our voice very well, we still need to know if it will be all right when there are several people in the room. One way to check this is to have someone stand at one end of the room with us at the other end and have them talk in a low voice. Not in a whisper, but in a conversational tone, as if they were talking to someone next to them, because that's what people do in meetings many times—they talk as though they were talking to someone next to them. If we can hear without any trouble, we can be a little more assured that things will be heard when the room is full. This matter of talking like they were talking to someone next to them is another of our problems. Even if the room is acoustically satisfactory for someone who talks in a normal voice, we can't regulate how low the participants will talk. If someone talks very low, and we know they will be in the meeting, we'd better make whatever plans we can to take care of the situation. *The rule is to prepare for the minimal conditions, not the normal or average conditions.*

Visibility is always a problem and one that can cause a good meeting to go sour. If the meeting is to be built around charts or movies or other visuals, and some of the people will not be able to see, then obviously they won't get much out of the meeting. But that's not the only problem. Even if the people are to be seated at a table and no visuals are to be used, they still like to see the speaker. This should be considered when the chairs are arranged, or the tables set out. Many meetings are ruined because all of the people are aligned along two sides of a table. Each time someone says something, everybody leans way over to try to see what is happening. Each has to lean out farther than the last, and pretty soon some are saying to themselves, "What's the use?"

Interference at a key point in the meeting can cause a near disaster, especially if we have spent valuable time building up our case. Just about the time we are making our final point, hoping now for concurrence from the group, the painter comes wandering through with a ladder swinging over the heads of all the people in the meeting. "Sorry folks, but this is the only way to get to the next room to finish up the paint job there!" While we weep, the group starts over to try to remember where they were a few minutes ago. Just as with acoustics, we can't check for interference just by standing in the middle of the room and listening one time. We have to know whether the room next door is being painted. We have to know what the hall sounds like when everyone on that floor takes a break and heads for the cafeteria at the same time. Is there a kitchen next door where dishes will be rattling at lunch period? Do they use a high-powered vacuum cleaner on the rugs every Friday morning? These types of interference are obvious, and the person conducting the session can avoid them with a little planning and checking. But there is another kind of interference that is much more subtle. There is the secretary who brings the boss a message, or calls the boss to the telephone, or tells the boss his or her plane tickets are ready. What's important is not *why* the secretary is there, but just the *fact* that he or she is. While only trying to be efficient, the secretary may be interrupting a number of work hours, and hurting the chances of success of the meeting. A note on the door, "Do Not Disturb," can help a lot, but arrangements for someone to take messages and deliver them at break periods is a much better guarantee. An extra sentence in the meeting announcement, "If you're expecting any messages during the meeting, have them left with my secretary at Ext. 7953," could solve the problem.

## CONDUCTING THE CONFERENCE

Interestingly enough, our role as leader may vary from meeting to meeting and even during any particular meeting. This is why it is so important to know just exactly what the purpose of the meeting is. If we know this, then we can more easily tell what our role is. Primarily, our function is to see that somebody takes all of the roles required to run a good meeting, which may mean that we will have to assume those not taken by others. If we are in charge of the meeting, the best thing we can do is to assign roles effectively to others. Put someone in the "initiating" role, someone else in the "timekeeping" role, try to get others to supply the "support" role, etc. This way we can keep up with what is going on and know when to step in and take over a role not being taken by someone else, or we can reassign roles that are not being taken very well by others. The thing to remember is that good leaders aren't necessarily seen and heard all of the time. Effective leaders simply see that everything runs smoothly, regardless of who is seen and heard the most. Most often we mistake the word "leader" to mean the person who stands on his or her feet or gives the direction or moves the meeting on to the next point. This may be us, or it may be someone we have assigned to the role because we know they have a lot of ability at that particular function.

### Hidden agendas

One interesting and frustrating thing about many meetings is that there often exist undercurrents of thoughts and needs and ideas and objectives that never quite get out into the open. These things have been called *hidden agendas*. Hidden agendas are simply those objectives that people bring to meetings that may differ from the real purpose of the meeting. Even though the stated purpose of the meeting may be to discuss overtime, we may really want to say a few things about work standards, and may even want to get some answers on the subject. As decisions are being made, we may appear to be basing our suggestions on just plain common sense, or the needs of the group, but we may have a hidden agenda that tells us that certain things would be more popular with the boss or make our department look better. It is difficult to pinpoint every agenda that is brought to the meeting by each member of the group, but at least we should be aware that they are bound to be there. We should also be aware that they will affect the meeting because they tend to produce biased answers. The first time we get an answer that surprises us because it doesn't sound reasonable in terms of the discussion so far, we might want to look and see if a hidden agenda is at work. We should ask ourselves, "What else could make Bob say that? Has he said something else before that indicates that there are forces working on him from back on the job? Is he trying to protect his job or his boss or his people?" The interesting thing is that we won't necessarily take any action to try to change the agenda Bob is working with; we'll just be sure to consider what he says in terms of what we think his needs are. The main thing is not to try to become a mind reader. We may never know exactly why people react the way they do—in fact, *they* may not even know—but if we see them beginning to fit a pattern, we should be alert enough to understand what they're doing and why. If we feel pretty sure that we know what's causing them to react the way they are, we may even make this work for us. If we have good reason to suspect that someone has a hidden agenda that will cause him or her to be very budget conscious, we direct toward that person ideas about things being cheap, and even draw him or her out on these items. On the other hand, we try to avoid getting such a person involved in matters that deal with cost increases. (We don't hide these matters, but we don't make great issues out of them, either.)

## Feedback

One of the things that tells us that hidden agendas exist in our group is the kind of *feedback* we get from the participants. Without the proper amount of feedback, we can't tell how the group feels, what individuals are thinking, what direction we should take, or how well we are doing at directing the conference toward its goal. But while it's pretty obvious *why* we need feedback, it isn't always obvious *how we get* it. Let's look at some ways of getting feedback, remembering that the purpose is to use the information toward controlling the meeting and reaching the objectives we have set.

If the group is small, it isn't too difficult to get the feedback. Usually a small group means less formality, hence everyone is saying what they think. At least it isn't hard to get the participants to answer a question directed to them, and they may even volunteer to give their opinions. As the size of the group increases, the problems of getting feedback increase. Now we have to use some techniques that will more or less force the participants to give us the feedback we need. This isn't so difficult, either, but it takes a little more effort. For example, we can simply go around the room and ask for comments on specific subjects. We can ask for a show of hands for both agreement *and* disagreement. (Be careful on this one. Even if no one raises a hand to show disagreement, it does *not* necessarily mean that everyone agrees. There are always those who won't hold up their hands but who still disagree. In this case we watch and see who doesn't hold up a hand for either yea or nay, then ask them how they feel. If nothing else happens, it will get them in the habit of responding one way or the other.) Since people coming to the meeting are supposed to be representing certain viewpoints, they aren't doing their job properly if they don't express themselves. We may have to help them along by asking direct questions, which we shouldn't hesitate to do. Remember, they are supposed to be there to help out, and embarrassing them isn't a problem. This doesn't mean that we *try* to embarrass them, but it does mean that we can ask them questions like "We haven't heard from you, Jean. What do you think about this matter?" Another technique we can use is to have the participants talk in small groups and report to the whole group. This way they iron out their differences in the small sessions, and not before the entire group. Often they just want to be sure they have had a chance to be heard, and are just as satisfied to do it before a small group as before the whole meeting. The leader can see that good ideas get out before the entire group by listening to the small subgroups and then, when the larger group re-forms, giving one member or another a cue such as, "Didn't I hear you saying that this wasn't really a problem in your office anymore?" Do this only when they fail to bring out the points you want brought out, of course. We don't ever want to suggest that we already know what we want them to say, and that if they don't say it, we'll do it for them. Nothing will kill their incentive any quicker.

What do we do with this feedback once we have gotten it? We use it to control and direct the meeting. We see where the participants are and how far along they are. If they aren't doing as well as we think they should be, we take steps to move along faster. If they are on schedule, we make note of it and keep on the same track. If they seem to be ahead of where we had thought they would be, we may even do some thinking about concluding the meeting early or planning on additional things we might undertake in the meeting. But that isn't the only function of the feedback. Here is a great way to get commitment. If we hear them say something that we want them to stand up for when they leave, we can have them emphasize it right in the meeting. "How about going over that again, Jim. I think that's the best way I've heard that put so far." Another use for feedback is to give us something to move on to the next subject with. When we have exhausted a subject and find it's time to go on, the ideal way is to do it by using some of the feedback: "O.K., Mona, that really takes us to the next subject, doesn't it? The way you have expressed it is . . ." The transition is smooth and we don't appear to be completely dominating the session. Mona gets credit for "initiating" something new, the group gets an introduction to what is going to be talked about, and we know things are running smoothly.

## Conflict

It would be unrealistic not to mention the fact that we can occasionally expect to run into some conflict in the meetings. Our first inclination when we meet conflict is to become a little frightened. We think conflict is bad and may ruin our fine meeting. Of course, too much conflict *can* ruin a meeting, but a certain amount should be expected and planned for. We've already seen that people have hidden agendas, so we shouldn't think that the meeting alone has caused the conflict. Also, when people feel strongly enough about something to cause conflict among themselves and others, that means they are involved and have some commitment on the subject being discussed. We should be glad this is the case, and try our best to use it to our advantage. First we need to be sure to recognize conflict when it comes up in the meeting. Snide remarks, digs at other conferees and other obvious things aren't hard to recognize as signs of conflict. More subtle signs are withdrawals, over-politeness, too-quick committal, and frequent efforts to go back and discuss topics that have obviously been closed. There is no reason ever to let conflict break out into open hostility such as name-calling, shouting, etc. We keep this from happening by stepping in before it gets this far. But what do we do when we step in? Do we just say, "Now let's not have any conflict"? Hardly. The best thing to do is to use the situation to our advantage by formalizing the debate, thus relieving some of the steam, or by trying to state the conclusions of each side, thus directing the attention away from the disagreeing participants and back to us. By restating the positions, and by even throwing in more facts, we can often resolve the conflict. But we may not want to resolve it too quickly. With it we have involvement, interest, and participation. Without it we may not have any of these things. When there is conflict, at least we know people are giving us their opinions. We also see others taking sides, thus committing themselves. We are, in a way, getting some of the best feedback we could hope for. As long as it is productive, let's keep it going. When we feel it has done all the good it can do, and may be starting to do some harm, we can step in and put a stop to it. We do this in a number of ways, either by taking a stand ourselves and asking for commitment from all concerned, or by gradually working our way into the conversation and turning it around to more productive fields. Another way, which is not the best but may be necessary, is to simply point out that while the situation is interesting, it probably isn't getting us very far. If conflict persists, we may have to postpone a portion of the meeting to a later date until the conflict can be resolved. Hopefully, the people engaged in the conflict will withdraw or give in some, so that postponement won't be necessary. Most often, the group as a whole will put enough pressure on the individuals so that the situation will work itself out and there needn't be another meeting.

## USING THE CONFEREES

Most people who are good at conducting meetings or conferences have learned a simple skill: they use the other conferees to help make the meeting a good one. *They share the leadership roles.* They recognize that it takes more than one person in a meeting to get the job done, so they don't just *allow* group members to assume various roles; they plan—and even manipulate—to get them into those roles. They've learned, for instance, that if somebody else does a good job of summarizing, let them do it. If somebody is conscious of the time and reminds the group about deadlines, the leader thanks the person for reminding them of the time factor and doesn't resent it at all. If somebody plays the "devil's advocate," asking questions and taking the opposite side to test the ideas being discussed, they let them do it because they need that role played and it's best played by one of the members. Good leaders know that when people participate in a meeting and think of it as their own, they'll be much more likely to support the results that come out of it.

   To best understand this, we have only to remember the last meeting we went to where the leader played all the roles. The *leader* kept us on track; the *leader* reminded us of the time; the *leader* interrupted the long-winded participant; the *leader* praised good ideas and questioned bad ones. The *leader* asked, "Will people really support that idea?" The *leader* negotiated compromise among varying positions and thoughts; the *leader* introduced new ideas when things began to wind down too soon; the *leader* brought out those who weren't talking or contributing. When we watch such a person, we might even think that he or she is doing a wonderful job. We might even think of patterning ourselves after this leader, thinking how nice it was to have everything under control. So what is wrong with this approach to conference leading? The problem is simple: It was never anybody's meeting but the leader's. Everyone let the leader have it, sat back and said, in essence, "What do you want me to do now?" They contributed only when they were told to and stopped when told to. They were supporting the LEADER, not the reason for the meeting. It never was THEIR meeting. The end product isn't theirs either. They won't be excited about how things go, and if things go wrong, they'll feel sorry for the leader, not for themselves and their effort.

Successful conferences, then, are the result of smart leaders sharing the meeting *and the purpose* with the conferees. They begin the planning with this in mind and never let up. It's always "*our* meeting." It's always "*we* need to solve this problem." When people are invited, they are often told what they can contribute that others can't and are urged to do so. When they arrive, each is greeted as a special person bringing ideas and solutions and ability to tackle the problem at hand. If some have something special to report, their names are on the agenda, and mention is made of it at the start to give them proper recognition. Roles may even be assigned—such as someone to take notes and someone to serve as timekeeper—to people who are willing to play those roles. The good leaders will observe people falling into certain roles and let them do so. If someone seems good at sensing the need for a compromise, and starts working toward that end, he or she is allowed to go ahead without interruption. A good leader will make a mental note of this, and will call on this person later if it seems a compromise needs to be worked out. The next time any of us attends a meeting, watch and see if the roles are being shared. It's entirely possible that a good meeting can run for its duration with the leader (the person *assigned* to the job) sitting back and doing very little. The best thing for us to do is try it ourselves. If we've been designated as the leader, we take it gladly, but during the meeting see if we can get others to play the roles we've talked about. Also see if this doesn't get more commitment from the people there.

Let's see how it might go in a meeting. The leader is Doug. The conferees include Debbi, Phil, and Blanche. Others are there, but we won't go into their roles. The meeting has been going on for awhile when we pick it up:

DEBBI: I don't think that's going to work at all. That idea has been tried before.

PHIL: Well, maybe not quite like I suggested. Besides, that was some time ago, and things have changed a lot since then. I think it'll work.

DEBBI: I can't see how. If we go out and make a proposal like that, they'll laugh us out of the place.

BLANCHE: Is there some way we can wrap it in a different wrapper?

PHIL: What do you mean, "a different wrapper"?

BLANCHE: If it's a good idea but people remember the old way we did it, call it by a different name, use a different approach, give it our endorsement, let people know we've put some thought into it.

PHIL: Well, that seems a little sneaky . . .

DEBBI: Hmmm. I see what you're saying, though, Blanche. It isn't the idea that's bad, just the reputation.

BLANCHE: That's right. As I hear you two talking about it, I think it's something that's pretty timely. It would be a shame if we lost the use of the idea just because at another time under different circumstances a similar idea didn't get the job done.

PHIL: I can't argue with that. And there are some changes that need to be made. I guess I agree with Debbi that a few of the things I've proposed could be improved on. Why don't we give it a try this way?

DEBBI: If we make the right changes, I think I'll be willing to give my support all the way.

So, what did we learn? Where was the leader? We never did hear from Doug. Why not? Simple. He wasn't needed. Things were going too well for him to mess it up by getting in and doing what the others were doing very well themselves. Note that there was some giving in, some compromising, some delving into history, some negotiating going on. There was a plan of action being developed. And more than anything else, there was some commitment going into the final product of the meeting.

This isn't to say that the leader couldn't and shouldn't have stepped in if things got out of control or if there didn't seem to be any direction. But when we have somebody like Blanche doing such a masterful job—perhaps without even thinking about it—we should stay out!

## LEADERSHIP ROLES

We've talked a lot about the leadership roles people play. Here's a brief summary of these roles and the part each plays. Think about them the next time a meeting comes along and see if anybody but the leader is playing them. In fact, let's see if we can play some of them when we're not the nominal leader. Not to take the role away from the leader, but to give all the help we can.

*Harmonizer:* Keeps the atmosphere friction-free; looks for points of agreement rather than stirring disagreement. Will recognize supporting statements from different participants and bring them out.

*Compromiser:* Will work for agreement by using trade-offs. Recognizes when people are willing to give in on certain points and which things they feel strongly about. Serves as moderator in negotiation.

*Conscience:* Reminds group of the goal and makes effort to keep them moving. May use chastisement to move toward the goal. Expresses discomfort when group is needlessly hung up on unimportant point.

*Gatekeeper:* Understands the process of moving a group off dead center. Will use techniques of questioning or repetition or reflection to get things going. Knows when group is ready to move to another point.

*Catalyst:* Asks creative and even uncomfortable questions to get group thinking. Will be able to bring in reticent participants by arousing emotions or getting them involved in in one of the issues.

*Summarizer:* Keeps group aware of where they are. Marks their progress with a summary or feedback on decisions. Recognizes when there is repetition or discussion on topics already settled and moves group on with a good transition statement. May take notes for group or even work at the easel to summarize.

## ENDING THE CONFERENCE

Just as it is important to know how to plan, start, and conduct a meeting, it is important to know how and when to end one. Why should this be a problem? Isn't everyone anxious to get out of the meeting and back on the job? Yes, probably so, but that's the trouble; we let them go before we have taken care of some important matters. For example, when it appears we have covered all necessary points and reached the proper solutions, we're ready to adjourn, aren't we? NO, not yet! Does the group *know* what the conclusions are? Do the people know what we have agreed to do and say? Do they know who's supposed to do what? These things have to be taken care of or all our efforts may go for naught. Maybe just a summary statement is all we need. "So this is what we've agreed to do: First we will tell . . ." By stating these things clearly and concisely, we are asking for commitment and consent. If we have watched the meeting closely, there shouldn't be any misunderstanding. But we state the agreements anyway, so there will be no doubts. But we also state the action we have planned and who it is that has the responsibility for taking care of the action. We make sure all participants understand their roles and are committed to carrying them out. If another meeting is required or some reporting period is necessary, this should be settled without doubt. If certain people are to finish certain actions before the next meeting, a schedule should be worked out and the timetable agreed upon. If we suspect that one or more of the people don't really know what they're supposed to do, or aren't committed, this is the time to get it straight. Once the meeting is over, it's going to be difficult to take care of these things.

## FOLLOWING UP ON THE MEETING

It would seem that after all that has been done so far to make this a successful meeting, surely there is nothing left to do. Maybe not, but don't be too sure. There are at least three things that need to be done before we can call it a completely successful session. First, we need to check on the action of all those who had things to do and deadlines to meet. Are they staying on schedule? Are they doing what the group at the meeting really decided on? Have they run into problems that were not anticipated? Just natural common sense tells us that we will need to do these things and find the answers to these questions. Secondly, we should report the action of the conference to those who need to be advised. The report need not necessarily be a long set of notes or minutes, but should contain enough infomation so that those who could not attend or who will be affected by the results will know what was done and what was planned. Finally, we need to take a look at the meeting as an effort to improve our own ability to conduct meetings. How did we do? Were there things that should have been handled differently? Will we make the same mistakes again, or do we see how we went wrong? Did we handle the conflict well? Did we recognize the support we were getting from some of the conferees? (And did we make use of it?) As new supervisors we may make some mistakes in conducting our first meetings; this is expected and acceptable. However, if we don't look at our actions and our mistakes with a view toward doing better the next time, our next mistakes are inexcusable!

## CONCLUSION

Someone has described a conference as a "meeting with a purpose." That's as good a definition as we can think of to describe the attitude we should have toward a conference. Some dread going to conferences; some dread conducting them. We should understand that the conference isn't just another meeting with no purpose, but rather, a gathering together of specific people for a specific purpose at a specific time. If we can't find the purpose of the conference, then by the definition we've just seen, it isn't a real conference. It's a purposeless collection of people who will waste the organization's time, and may even make insignificant decisions about unimportant things. When we put an announced purpose on the gathering, it becomes a full-fledged conference and deserves all the attention we can give it to make it a success. And that's what it takes to make a conference a success: *all the attention we can give it.* Good conferences aren't measured by how well we handled the "talkers" or how close we came to the announced quitting time— but by their results. True, how we handled the conference will have some effect on the results, but there's a lot more to it than that. Results will depend on how well the conference was planned, how well we did in selecting conferees, how well they understood and played their roles in the conference, and how well we did in sharing the various functions of conference leading. If we ended up playing all the roles, from gatekeeper to summarizer, *we* may have had a good conference but it's doubtful that anyone else did.

The logic behind a good conference is pretty simple. "Conference" implies a group of people *conferring.* The process goes like this: We select some people to come together to confer because a problem exists and they are the people who are concerned with the problem or who have some information that will help in solving that problem. Our job as conference leader is to use those people in such a way that there won't be a problem after we've had the conference or after we carry out the action decided on by the people attending. This means that we use these resources to do what they can do best: solve the problem at hand. If further action is required, we make sure to get their commitment to the solution by involving them in both the strategy of problem-solving and the necessary action. As we said in Chapter 6, on planning and organizing, the planning isn't complete until the plan has been acted upon. We should never leave a conference without all participants knowing exactly what is expected of them, and when they are to complete what they have agreed to do. Finally, it is important that there be the followup we mentioned. See to it that they do their part. That's *our* part!

## EXERCISES

1. Individual activity: Have each member of the group think of the last meeting he or she went to. Try to pinpoint the date, who attended, and what the purpose was. They should be thinking of an actual meeting, not just remembering past meetings they've attended. Once they've picked a specific meeting, they should make a list of the things that helped the meeting to go well, and the things that kept it from running well. They should set up their paper as follows:

| Things that helped | Things that hindered |
|---|---|
| 1. | 1. |
| 2. | 2. |
| etc. | etc. |

2. Group activity: When the individuals have finished exercise 1, they should report it and have it recorded. This will give rather long lists of things that help and things that hinder the success of a meeting. These lists are valuable, and each person should keep a copy of them for future use. For now, though, let the group decide what the conference or meeting leader could do to overcome the "hindrances" that are listed. Many of them are obvious, like set an agenda, set starting and stopping times, etc. Others are more subtle.

These, too, should be listed on the board and made a part of the observers' permanent notes.

3. Group activity: Again looking at the list generated from exercise 1, have the group discuss how many of the hindrances could have been overcome by the *participants,* apart from whatever the leader could have done. Brainstorm a list of things participants can do in any meeting to make it better, even if the leader isn't doing a very good job.

4. Individual activity: Each person should think of a meeting he or she will be having in the near future. It may be a large one or simply a staff meeting with a few people attending. Take a few minutes and answer the following questions:

> What is the purpose of the meeting?
>
> What is the expected product?
>
> Who should attend?
>
> When should they be notified?
>
> How should they be notified?
>
> Are some people more important to the meeting than others?
>
> Is seating arrangement important—and if so, how will they sit?
>
> Can I assign certain leadership roles to some of the people—and if so, to whom?
>
> What time is the meeting scheduled?
>
> What time should it be over?
>
> How much leeway have I got?

(This information need not be fed back to the entire group. Small subgroups can review one another's responses and compare their progress.)

# 12
# PROBLEM-SOLVING

Problem-solving, like most of the other things discussed thus far, is a skill. There are specific steps in the process which, when properly followed, pretty well guarantee success. The difficulty often comes when we start to look at the process, because the steps *sound* complicated. Actually, the process is simple and is the one we use most of the time in our personal decisions. When we consider buying a car, a house, or a boat, we go through these steps. We don't necessarily go through them *consciously,* but we deal with each of them nevertheless. As we discuss the steps, then, it's a good idea to think about how we use them in solving our everyday problems. If we already use the process, one might ask, why talk about it here? Well, because we use the process or its steps on *big* problems, but not on the small ones that often can grow into big ones if they aren't handled correctly. Also, there seems to be some reason why we don't always make the application to the job, even though we use the ideas in our own affairs. (For example, we realize that we quite often have to resort to buying things on credit—and in the process end up paying more money for them—but we fail to see that the organization we work for runs into the same problem; i.e., not enough cash to pay now and save money later.)

The suggestion here is to start developing the habit of using the specific steps on small items until we automatically go through the steps in any problem situation. We will look at the steps, see how they work, give some examples, and leave it up to the supervisor to make the application on his or her own. Again, let's emphasize: The steps just *sound* complicated; they aren't really all that hard to understand and apply!

## DEFINING THE PROBLEM

The first step in problem-solving is to be sure we are attacking the *right problem.* An employee comes to us and claims to be tired of working on a certain job. If we take that at face value and start to solve that

problem, we may find that we are solving the wrong problem, and maybe creating another. In reality, the employee may be fed up with us as a supervisor, or have had about all he or she can take from the employee who works across the aisle, or be making more mistakes than necessary because he or she hasn't had enough training.

How do we know whether we are trying to solve the right problem? The best way is to do what the doctor does when examining a patient—get all the symptoms together and see what kind of picture develops. This way we won't be treating just a symptom, but the real problem. Once we identify the symptoms we start to ask "What are the things that could produce these symptoms?" If employees are doing poor work, that may be a symptom of poor attitudes which may be a symptom of poor supervision or perhaps poor working conditions. Are there other signs, such as high turnover rates, absenteeism, tardiness, etc.? Are some of the employees performing all right while others aren't? Have these same employees performed better in times past? Only after we have satisfied ourselves with the answers to these questions can we be sure we are solving the correct problem and not just treating a symptom. Once we are sure we know what the problem is, it's a good idea to state it for our own clarification. "Reduce loss of production time. Reduce the error rate. Increase the overall production rate for the group." Note that it's *not* the time to say, "Reduce the error rate caused by union intervention." This assumes that we already know the cause of the problem, which may be the case, but it's a good idea to get a few more facts before stating this. This brings us to the next step in the problem-solving process.

## GATHERING INFORMATION

The information stage is an important one, but one that's often taken too lightly. After all, we've spent all this time defining the problem, haven't we got enough information? No, not at this stage. We aren't ready to solve the problem yet. We just want to get as much information as we can to help us be sure we really are solving the right problem, then to help us pick up some ideas on how to solve the problem. Once we've gathered as many facts as seem to be available *in the time allowed us to look,* we take one last look and see if we really are on the right track. Have we discovered that every supervisor before us has had the same problem with the same employees on the same job? This doesn't make the problem go away, but it does change the complexion of the problem.

Note that we emphasized getting as many facts as time allows. One of the important decisions that supervisors must be able to make is to know when to stop looking and start solving. In other words, we must recognize that to go any further would take more time and effort than the problem deserves. We might like to have production records going back for ten years, but if such information would take weeks of digging by a number of employees, we need to be able to measure its value against the cost of obtaining it. On the other hand, if the information is available right in the files, we can't use the excuse, "It'll take too long to get the information." Note, again, we aren't looking for a solution yet, so that any information should be gathered with an open mind. It would be improper of us to gather only that information that will help us prove a point, rather than solve the real problem. If we go into the problem-solving process with preconceived notions of what we are going to do anyway, then following specific procedures is just useless exercise.

It is essential, during this information-gathering stage, that we get specific information, rather than generalities. We need to find out things like who or what, how many, how much, where, when, how long, etc. We will find that this kind of information is harder to get than general comments, but much more reliable in the long run. For example, it's not enough to have statements like "She's late all the time." We need to ask, "How many times in the last month?" We shouldn't accept information like "This machine is costing us a fortune in repair bills." Such information will sink our argument one of these days. If we don't ask it, our boss might: "How much is a fortune?" Admittedly, generalities and opinions are much easier to get, and we probably make more friends when we ask their opinions instead of making them dig up *specific* information. But we are trying to solve a *specific* problem; hopefully, we are going to recommend that *specific* action be taken. If all of this is based only on opinions, then we aren't likely to have the best solution available. By the way, when we're getting this information, we should make some kind of mental or written note on just how reliable the information really is. If some information is questionable, we should so note it, because otherwise we may find ourselves making decisions on that information just as if it were completely reliable. If we know that there is some doubt as to the validity of the information, we'll treat it with caution later on. If not, we may forget and create for ourselves a little grief that could easily have been avoided.

## FINDING THE CAUSE

The reason we have stressed so hard the fact that we aren't yet ready for the solution is that at this point we are ready to identify the *cause*. Only when we have found the cause can we select an appropriate solution. Using the information we have gathered, we look at all the possible causes. If we decide that the cause of the poor work output is the result of inadequate training, not poor work habits, then we have some valuable data to use toward applying the proper solution. However, we may find that we will need more information or a different kind of information to get rid of the cause.

The difficult thing to remember is that causes aren't always easy to find. Rather than say that the cause isn't obvious, we should say that the cause that is obvious may not be the real problem. If we have a problem because one of the workers in the office is being snippy with people in other departments, the cause may not be his or her bad attitude; it may be that we haven't made the assignment completely clear, and the worker is protecting his or her job in what seems to be the safest way—by keeping others away from it. An employee who is afraid that the job he or she has is not as important as other jobs will do his or her best to make it seem that way, even if it comes out as trying to make life miserable for other people. "I'm sorry, but I'm too busy to help right now," or "Did the boss tell you to handle that? That's my job and I don't want you messing it up." The cause may be poor supervision, poor definition of work responsibility, inadequate work, or several other things. But if we've gotten enough information, we should have a pretty good idea at this stage just what the real cause of the problem is.

After we are sure we have the cause isolated, it's still a good idea to take a quick check of past history. Did this same thing cause the same problem at some other time? Has this same problem been caused by a shift change or cutover to new equipment before? Have we always had this problem when we put in new equipment? There are a couple of good reasons for checking past history when we have identified the cause. First, has someone identified this as a cause before and tried to solve the problem by eliminating the cause? Did the problem go away? Did it turn out to be more expensive to solve than the solution was worth? Did it turn out to be only part of the solution? Are the basic ingredients still there; that is, the same people, the same office, the same equipment? If they are, did the solution just fail to take effect or has something else—some new ingredient—entered into the picture?

The second good reason for checking history is to find out if there is any record of the problem *going away by itself.* Some problems are that way. When there is a change in the office routine, trouble develops. We know we should do something but aren't sure just what. Then before we know it the problem has disappeared! The danger in this kind of thinking is that most of us tend to expect that *all* problems will go away sooner or later. This just isn't so. Many potentially good supervisors have fallen by the wayside waiting for the problems to disappear. Even many problems that seem to leave come back in another form— often a much more horrible form at that. So we can't wait just because some problems do go away. But we can find out if this particular problem is caused by this particular thing that has a history of repeating itself, then going away. For example, when it's time to replace a typewriter in the office, we can be sure that there will be someone who isn't happy with your selection of who gets the new one, no matter how fair your decision is. (Employees don't always want fairness—they sometimes want new typewriters!) A check with supervisors who have been around for awhile will tell us what to expect when the new typewriter decision is made. This same check may tell us that it's all right that some of the employees are miffed; they always are, and it will wear off by itself. If we are satisfied that this is right, and that the new typewriter caused the problem, then we can be equally satisfied that time will heal the problem just as well as any other solution we pick. Of course, if we know enough about the situation before we select the new typewriter or the person getting it, we may do some things to keep the problem from arising.

## FINDING ALTERNATIVE SOLUTIONS

Now comes the tricky stage where we have already determined the cause, and are going to try to find the best solution, the solution that will eliminate whatever is causing the problem. The reason this is tricky is that it is the last time we can really use much imagination or inge- nuity. What we want to do now is to think of several possible solutions, not just one. We want the *best* one and there is a way of getting it. The process is to *brainstorm,* that is, to think of as many alternatives or options as possible without making any efforts to evaluate them, or decide on one, or throw any of them out as not being feasible. The most important thing is that we must not allow ourselves to think, "Well, I'm sure that won't work, so I'll rule it out now." About the only rule is to concentrate on those solutions that will most likely re- move the cause we have located. If there is doubt, *keep the idea around* anyway, unless the doubt is very strong. (We might even ask ourselves, "Why did we think of this in the first place? There must be some reason it came to mind, so I'd better keep it for awhile.")

The problem with evaluating too early is that we may overlook some good ideas by just not getting around to thinking about them! We hit on an idea that sounds good and we go with it, thereby never even thinking of alternatives that may have been better in the long run. To make it worse, the idea we picked to solve our problem may end up being less effective than hoped, either because it had some flaws in it, or wasn't as practical as it sounded to us in the beginning. By the time we find it out, we may have used up too much time or gone too far to consider other options. We may even find ourselves committed to this one and have to support it knowing it isn't the best possible solu- tion to our problem.

After we have spent some time listing (either mentally or on paper) all the ideas that we can think of, we should take a last look at them and see if anything else comes to mind. This will tell us if we've paid too much attention to just a single line of thought. Often ideas cause us to think of other ideas, so the time may be well spent. By the way, this is a good place to ask, "How do we know when we have enough options to choose from?" The answer is that we have to look at the problem and decide *how much time it's worth.* The bigger the problem, or the more complex it is, the more time can be devoted to solving it.

Two things are sure: We can spend too much time by just going on looking for more alternatives, and we can be pretty sure that we will reach the saturation point on productive ideas after awhile—in other words, we reach a point when the same amount of time no longer produces the same quality of alternative.

An advantage of listing the options we have looked at is that at some point when we are trying to justify the solution we chose, we can say "Well, I considered these other options but here is why I chose this one." If we have done a good job of thinking out our decisions, we can show why the way we took is better than the ones we rejected. Of course, if for some reason there is a need to take one of the other options (company policy, budget considerations, etc.), then it's also good to be able to say, "I considered that also, and if we go that route, then here are the things that will have to be done . . ." A final advantage is that it's sometimes possible to sell an idea by showing what the alternatives are. If someone doesn't like what we have chosen, it's good to be able to say that the alternatives are thus and so. It's just a lot better for us to list the options than for someone else to ask, "Why haven't you considered this . . .?" It weakens our decisions if we have to say that there are things we haven't considered, even if they turn out later to be bad alternatives.

## PICKING A SOLUTION

Now that we've gone through all of this, how do we go about picking the best solution from the options we have listed? There are some definite steps and we need to consider them now. First, we need to use a *systematic* approach. It would be a shame to go this far in such a careful manner and then lose all of the advantage by not using the same careful approach in picking the best alternative. The approach should be a screening process to look at each of the options we have picked and see if they meet certain criteria. If so, then we can use them; if not, then we can begin to eliminate them one by one.

First, we ask ourselves if the alternative we are looking for is really *possible*. We said earlier that we didn't want to rule out any ideas at that point, but now we begin to be very critical. Now is the time when we decide whether or not the idea really will work. Is it within the capability of our group, our talents, our budget? Next, we ask ourselves if the alternative is really *workable*. Even if we have the capabilities, will it really work under the conditions that exist in *our* work situation? Will our people accept the idea? Will this option fit into our way of doing things, considering the routine, our interfacing with other work groups, etc? Then we ask ourselves whether the alternative we are considering is really a *probable* solution. After all is said and done and we are ready to use it, are we willing to stick our necks out and pull for this as a solution? Will the boss accept the idea? In other words, what is the *probability* that the idea will work and will be used? Finally, we ask the obvious question: Is the idea *applicable* to this problem at this time under these circumstances?

This last question is the most critical of all. We must be sure that the solution applies to the real problem, the one we finally settled on in the beginning. As we study the alternative to see whether or not to use it, we want to know not only whether or not it applies to the specific problem, but whether it solves *all* of it? We should be comfortable with an alternative that gets this far in the testing, and we will be if we are sure it fits the problem and will solve all of it. Because of the systematic approach we have used, we have eliminated most of the "bad" solutions by now. The way to evaluate the ones that are left is to put them to one more test. We have, of course, placed certain "must" conditions on each of these solutions. Any option we picked had to meet these musts. But as a consequence, we also find that they meet certain "nice" conditions, some more than others. We have said that we realize that we can't expect everything, but there are things that would be nice to have while we are using the option we chose. One way to pick the best alternative, once we have found those that get this far, is to look at the "nice" benefits we get from each one. Those that meet all of the "musts" and provide the most or best "nice" items become the most attractive to us. It is from this list that we pick the final solution. Stated simply, we pick the one that not only will solve the problem we have stated, but also will give us the best side benefits. We have to be careful here, though, because we don't want to become attached to an idea just for its side benefits. We could end up defending it beyond its merit, when another option might solve the problem just as well, be more popular with other people, and perhaps be the most practical one to pick, *all because of some side benefit we feel so strongly about.*

Once we have chosen an alternative, and it has been checked out according to the suggestions here, we need to *state it very clearly.* For the benefit of all concerned we should make sure that everyone who hears about the solution knows exactly who is going to do what and what it will take in terms of people, money, and time. If we have decided to move certain people to new locations, we should specify which people, where they will go, and what will be their job responsibilities when they get there. If we have decided to go into overtime, we should state how much overtime will be required, who will work it, and how much it will cost. Remember, early in this chapter we said that this would sound complicated, but really isn't—so all of this doesn't have to be put down in elaborate form. Once those concerned have been told, the information should simply be available if someone asks. It can be in our minds *if we really have thought out the problem.*

## PUTTING THE PLAN TO WORK

This brings us to the point of implementing the solution. How do we go about introducing the new idea? Surely this shouldn't be a problem. It often is, though, and many plans fall through at this point. Again, certain questions must be asked. We have to anticipate problems and try to decide ahead of time how we will handle them. For example, we should ask ourselves, "Who will likely resist this solution?" If we anticipate that one of the old line workers will try to kill the idea, we should take steps to prevent this, even if it means going to that worker and getting him or her to help introduce it or give us some suggestions on ways to make it work. We need to decide what risks are involved in trying this new or different idea, and who will likely misunderstand what we are trying to do. Is our boss in agreement? Will he or she back us up when questions arise or opposition appears? After we've tried to anticipate who will be affected and what problems this will cause, we should see whether all risks, resistance, and resentments are covered. If so, it's time to carry out the plan we've chosen. Before we do that, we need to assure ourselves that we know what we're talking about. Going through these steps should give us the confidence to go ahead with the solution to the problem. We mention this at this point for two reasons: First, as new supervisors, we aren't always accepted for what we know or do. We are still thought of as new and thus not capable of thinking the great thoughts that others with more time and experience can think. While this isn't true, it doesn't keep people from feeling that way, so it has to be considered. Second, we should not be afraid to push our ideas. By going through the steps we've discussed, we have become very familiar not only with the problem, but also with the alternatives for solving it. In a way, we have become experts on this small portion of the operation, and this should overcome the lack of confidence that others have in us and that we have in ourselves. This is pretty important to the outcome of the project!

## CARRYING OUT THE PLAN

Now comes the important part of making our plan operate. We have spent valuable time arriving at what we think is the best solution to the problem. We have confidence that it is going to work. But it won't work by itself! If the plan is poorly carried out or not done according to the way we've specified, the results will make the solution *look* like the wrong one, even if it's not. Surely the solution deserves as much careful attention in the work stage as it did in the selection and planning stage.

Carrying out the plan means more than just putting it to work, or telling someone else to do the job. It means keeping track of the progress, watching how well things are going, even making adjustments along the way. We must be careful to avoid being so committed to the plan that we can't see things that are going wrong. Our commitment should be to the *job,* not our plan. Again, this doesn't mean that we have to spend a lot of time sitting around watching everything that happens. If we have confidence in the plan, we should be able to let it run its course fairly well. But occasional spot checking should tell us if we are really solving the problem. If we have reassigned some of the workers to different jobs, then we can tell a great deal by looking at production figures on a sampling basis. If the sales territory has been changed, then occasionally checking the present results with previous ones will tell us all we need to know about the plan we are trying out.

While we are watching the plan in operation, it's a good idea to keep an eye out for potential trouble. We've already talked about making a note on where we might expect opposition or misunderstanding. Since we know this ahead of time, we have some good check points. The trick is to know when trouble is brewing so we can head it off, not wait until things are in bad shape to step in. The skill of anticipating trouble is a hard but valuable one to learn. Most trouble can be stopped more easily when it first starts than after it's gone on awhile. If we suspect that someone is going to misunderstand or not like the solution we are instituting, we'd better make sure that they don't get too many opinions formed before we deal with their misunderstandings. It will be a lot harder to change their minds than it will be to help them make up their minds in the first place.

Part of the reason for watching the progress of our solution is to check on our own problem-solving ability. We will need to know— sometime in the future—just how well we did at defining the problem, selecting alternatives, and picking the right option. Not only will we want to know how well we did at this, but we will want to get a look at the *value* of the solution. As we think about our future problem-solving efforts, we will want to ask ourselves, "Was all of this done efficiently, or did I spend a lot of time coming up with a solution that is now falling apart at the seams? Further, did I do a poor job of anticipating where the trouble would come from?" All of this leads us to the final step, that of following up on the solution after the plan has been put to work and all the smoke has cleared.

## FOLLOWING UP ON THE SOLUTION

The simple question we ask now is, "Did the solution really work?" The answer will tell us most of what we want to know. No matter how well-thought-out the plan was or how well we implemented it, if it didn't solve the problem, it really wasn't very good. But if it worked and we got the side benefits we thought we would get, then we'd have to say that the solution was a good one. If possible, we should try to find out *why* the solution worked. This may seem strange, but there is always the possibility that the problem disappeared in spite of what we did, rather than because of it. All this means is that we look and try to determine whether other factors were at work at the same time which may have had an effect on the outcome of the problem-solving effort. While this isn't worth a lot of time, it's worth at least a little to keep us from getting caught thinking we have solved a problem by ourselves when what someone else did had as much to do with the outcome as what we did.

As we mentioned earlier, we should always be looking for flaws in the solution. How might we have avoided the negative things that happened? Were there obvious signs that we missed, or was the error unavoidable? Would it have been worth the extra time to look longer for possible trouble? This is simply hindsight, but it's valuable. It can help us avoid making the same mistakes twice. It can help us measure our own ability at problem-solving. It can be of help to future problem-solvers, because if we have a good idea of what happened, they can learn from both our successes and failures. Of course, all of this presupposes that the problem is dead, not just sleeping. Sometimes problems disappear for awhile just because we have done something different; then, as soon as things settle down, they creep up on us again.

Part of following up on the solution includes finding out just exactly how much it took to make the solution work. How much did it really cost? How much overtime did we really put in that was directly related to our solution? Is the job actually *more* complicated as a result of our action? These are fair questions to ask and we may well need the information to support our next idea. If we have exceeded our estimated expenditure, it's a lot better for us to catch it than for someone else to. Also, when we find out exactly what the costs were in terms of money, material, and people, we can honestly answer the question *"Was it worth it?"* This can be done only when all the facts and figures are in.

## CONCLUSION

In the beginning of this chapter we said that the process seems complicated. What we have tried to do is give the complete layout for an approach to problem-solving. It will be a rare day when we use each of these steps in its full extent. No matter. The idea is to see that the approach to problem-solving is systematic, and not haphazard. Breaking it down into steps, as we have done here, shows more clearly that there is a beginning, a middle, and an end. The middle is only one step, picking a solution. What comes before and after determines how well the solution we pick is going to work. Briefly, here are the steps as they have been given:

1. Defining the problem
2. Gathering information
3. Finding the cause
4. Finding alternative solutions
5. Picking a solution
6. Putting the plan to work
7. Carrying out the plan
8. Following up on the solution

It wouldn't hurt us to write these down and paste them somewhere around our desk. When we start on a problem to solve, we can take a look at the list and ask "Where am I right now in the problem-solving process?" If we can't decide where we are, we'd better not be too confident of our solution. But if we're lucky (or just happen to be doing a good job) we can find out right where we are in the process and continue in full assurance that we're heading down the right road. We should have no fear that our solution will not be the right one!

## EXERCISES

1. Subgroup activity: Using the steps in problem-solving shown at the end of this chapter, go through the following problem, working in small groups of no more than four people.

   "Bill John is an accountant with a large firm. For some time now he has been doing some 'free-lance' work on the side, keeping books for small businesses and doing tax returns. He has a chance to do a job in a distant city next Saturday, a drive of about 90 miles. The Johns have two cars, one with automatic shift and the other with a standard shift. His wife, Betty, never learned to drive a standard shift, so she drives the automatic and he drives the standard. The standard needs new tires for road driving; but the old ones still have 'in-town' miles left on them. The automatic has new tires but they won't fit on the standard. It is Thursday when Bill finds out about the job in the distant city. When he calls his wife to tell her about it, he asks her what she has planned, if anything, for Saturday. Her reply is that she plans to take the new neighbor, Sally Thorne, shopping."

   At this point, we'll stop and let the subgroups work on the problem. When each group is finished, they should read out their answers to the entire group. A record of the answers should be kept.

2. Group activity: Using the same information as above, determine what we *don't* know in order to adequately solve the problem. How much information would be required to actually solve the problem? Suppose we were to find out that Sally Thorne doesn't have a car. Would this help us? And suppose we find out that the local bus doesn't go to the shopping center on Saturday? We still don't have all the information. What is needed? Have the group brainstorm exactly what we need to know in order to adequately bring the problem to a conclusion. (It's interesting how many might have suggested going ahead and buying the tires for the other car as a solution. While this has some merit, it's the kind of thing we do often in problem-solving if we don't have all the information we need—which many times is the case!)

# 13
# ORAL AND WRITTEN PRESENTATIONS

As supervisors, we find ourselves having to present solutions to problems we have solved or communicate our ideas up or down the line. We may do this either orally or in writing. In either case, the acceptance of the message can depend as much on the quality of our writing or speaking as on the message itself. It's too bad that we sometimes lose an argument or get poor results because we fail to do well at putting it in writing or standing in front of people speaking. Obviously we can't become great writers or speakers by reading one chapter in a book. But we can take a look at what we're *really* trying to do when we write or speak. Before going further, though, it would be a good idea to review the chapter on communications (Chapter 5), because we will need to apply some of the basics of communications in order to understand what is said here.

## WATCH STEREOTYPES

Perhaps the most common mistake we make in trying to improve our writing or speaking is to assume that there is just one right way to write or speak. We fail to realize that there are many acceptable ways to express ourselves. In writing, we can say what we say in several quite acceptable ways, and still reach our audience. We search for the correct form to use in writing a letter, for example, not realizing that anyone who says that there is only one way to set up a letter is misinformed. In fact, if we stick to some kind of stereotyped form in our writing, we may be stereotyping *ourselves*. We may be saying that we have no imagination, or that we are very formal, even when the occasion calls for an informal approach. We may be giving the impression that we are stodgy or old-fashioned, and that we lack the "looseness" required to suit a particular situation. Whether in speaking or writing, there is plenty of room for imagination, which means that the person

who always says something just a certain way or appears to be just the perfect orator may not be the best communicator. In fact, the polished orator will probably be out of place in the kind of speaking situations the supervisor gets into. There is really just one basic standard for writing or speaking: *Get the message across.*

There is a three-point plan of action that never fails. If we know these three things, we should be able to meet any kind of situation in which we are trying to get a message to someone else, whether by speaking or writing. They are:

1. Know your subject
2. Know your audience
3. Know yourself (capabilities)

Let's look at each of these and see what they mean to us as supervisors.

### Know your subject

What does it mean to know the subject? It means we should research it until we are sure we have a complete understanding of what we are about to write or say. Even if we aren't expected to be experts, we should at least know enough to see that our words and phrases are used correctly. This doesn't mean that we research it to death. It means that we simply learn as much as we are supposed to know, plus perhaps a little extra (but never a little less). Of course, if we are looked on as an expert and others are looking to us for all the answers, then we do, in fact, have to do a great deal of research. Perhaps a better way to look at it is to know what is important and what isn't. Rather than becoming an expert on a whole subject, we figure out what part is important to the audience or the reader and concentrate on that. We may even have to educate the audience to the fact that certain things *are* important. We also figure out what part is important to the project we're working on. Maybe the audience is interested in more information than the project requires. Maybe they think it would be interesting to pursue some things that really aren't pertinent to solving the problem at hand or that do not contribute to the overall project. If so, we simply have to avoid the trap and get to the important points, even though our audience thinks it wants something else. Of course, this means we must explain why we are leaving other things out, and be ready to defend our position. But the audience isn't all that causes us to add to the information we cover. We have our own pet subjects and like to ride certain horses to death every time we get a chance, so we have to control ourselves as well.

One of the best ways to regulate ourselves and our audience is to be familiar with the subjects that relate to the one we're writing or speaking about. Not that we have to become expert—just have enough knowledge so we can tell how some of the related material might affect the outcome of the project being discussed, or so that we can answer some of the questions that might be asked later. We shouldn't pose as an expert. We shouldn't try to bluff on the subject. We should simply try to familiarize ourselves with enough of the information to give us a pretty good picture of those things that relate to the subject at hand. (Later on, as we grow, we can take on more and more related subjects, but in the beginning it's better to be good at what we're talking about than to try to spread ourselves too thin.) Organization is the key here, because as we begin to organize and close up loose ends, we see where related subjects fit in, and where the weak spots are.

### Know your audience

Knowing the audience isn't as simple as it might appear. As we've already said, if what we want them to have differs from what they think they need, then we've got to tell them *in terms that are meaningful to them.* Even though we're expressing our own thoughts and ideas on the subject, the way we express them must be in terminology the audience will understand. Ideally, we should start off by making it clear that what the audience is getting is what it has asked for. This way at least the members are tuned in, whether they're getting the information exactly as they expected it or not. The way to appeal to the reader or listener is the same: "Here is the information you asked for." "You asked me to speak on . . ." At least we ought to start by saying, "You will be glad to know . . ." Whatever we do, we should use the name of our reader or listener, and second person, rather than *I* or *me.* This helps keep it friendly, especially if we avoid stock phrases such as "Enclosed please find . . . ," or "A funny thing happened on the way to make this speech . . ." Using phrases like this may say something about us that we don't want said. *And stopping is just as important as starting.* Nothing can be kinder or friendlier than stopping when we have said all we have to say. But if we aren't careful we fall back into some bad habits. "If I can be of further help to you in this or any other matter, please do not hesitate to call on me," and, "In closing, let me reiterate what I've already said . . ." These often kill whatever good might have been accomplished.

### Know yourself

The most important thing to know is ourselves. What are our capabilities? If we have the ability to talk and write on a subject, we shouldn't sell ourselves short. We're writing or speaking because we know enough about the subject to do just that, and that's reason enough. We also have a chance to sell ourselves, and that's an opportunity we should take advantage of. We also have a chance to prove a point that we've come up with. It may be a solution or an idea, and whatever it is, if we have done the research, we should not be willing to let someone else try to explain it just because we think we lack the ability to do so. It's often true that good ideas go down the drain because we fail to take advantage of the opportunity to sell them ourselves. We either let the idea go altogether or entrust it to someone else, who may lack the whole story or the interest to sell the idea.

But we also need to know our limitations. Even if we are willing to make the speech or write the letter, we should speak or write within our abilities. If we can't tell jokes, we shouldn't try. Use a substitute, such as a short anecdote from the newspaper, or just play it straight— that nearly always works! If we can't be an orator, we shouldn't try.

We should just tell it simply, quickly, and stop when we're through. If we aren't familiar with certain words or phrases, we leave them alone. We're better off not using them than using them incorrectly. And if we aren't sure about them, what about our audience? But just as we need to know our limitations, we need to do something about them. We should be constantly striving to do better than the last time. Each time we write or speak, it's a good idea to add one new challenge or trick of the trade. Try a little humor, add a dash or semicolon to our letter. When someone says, "You did a fine job," determine to do even better next time. If we feel we didn't do too well, decide what we did wrong and then look for an opportunity to try to do better, not just stop with a failure.

Note that skillful communication is pretty important to the new supervisor. The ability to express oneself in writing or by speaking before a group is an asset that never goes out of style. At every level in the organization we are called upon to tell someone something. *The telling is just as important as the finding out what to tell.* Very few things will call attention to ourselves and to what we know like the ability to say it or write it. A good oral briefing or a crisp, accurate report is an exciting thing to those who are short on time and need to get their facts in a hurry. If we are able to provide them with this service, we will certainly be rewarded for it. The higher we go in the organization, the more useful this skill becomes, so the better we get, the more we improve our likelihood of going higher up. Chances are pretty good that whenever two near-equals are being considered for a job, the one who can communicate better will win out.

## TIPS ON WRITING

Generally there are just three reasons why we ever write anything: to *inform,* to *request,* and to *substantiate* or document. When we write to inform, we are doing so because someone needs some information we have and has asked us to supply it, or we have some information they should be using and we want them to have it. As we mentioned earlier, they may not know they need it and we may have to sell them on accepting it, but at least we need to recognize that a particular letter is for the purpose of giving someone some information. Writing to request information is quite different from writing to give information. Our approach is different in that we have to be much more specific to be sure to get just what we need. Even in requesting information there are two reasons why we want it. First, we want it because we are going to use it; second, we want it because someone has asked us to get it for them. In the first case, we have only to determine exactly what we want and why we want it, then ask for it. In the second case, it's a little harder. We have a communications problem at both ends. We not only have to fathom someone else's needs and make sure we aren't asking for the wrong thing, but we also have to be sure we are getting it in good, usable form. This means we have the problem of deciding what the users are going to do with the information. If they are going to use it exactly as we get it to put into a report, then we must make sure to give it to them in near final form. If they're going to extract parts of the information and use it with other information, then we need to put it in a form that allows them to find things in it very quickly. Then, of course, we have the job of communicating this need to the people we are getting the information from, hence another communications problem. The third reason for writing is to substantiate or document a conclusion or decision we have made. In this case we have to be sure to use all the rules of good communicating, because we are really in the selling business now. This is especially true if we are writing to substantiate someone else's idea or conclusion. This happens when the boss tells us to "Write a letter to the client and tell him (or her) what we have decided on this matter."

So we have three reasons for writing: to *inform,* to *request,* and to *substantiate.* It's a simple thing to find out which reason we are writing for, but too many times we forget to do it. It's much easier to find the right words if we know why we are writing. It's also easier to proofread our writing when we know exactly why we're writing in the first place. We say to ourselves, "Did I make it perfectly clear what I wanted, or does the reader have to guess and read between the lines? Did I spend so much time leading up to the subject that the reason for writing got lost?" It's always a good idea to put ourselves in the reader's shoes and see if we can decide what the letter or report is all about. The simplest way to check our writing is to see if we got to the point quickly. It's just as bad to put in too much background information as to put in too little. If we spend too much time leading up to the reason for writing, the reader may have left us before we get to it. The best way is to open up with the purpose of the letter:

"Here's the answer on the framus machine you asked for . . . "

"Can you tell us how many of these you will need in the next year?"

"We recommend cancelling the project immediately . . ."

With lead-in sentences like these, the reader won't have to guess why we're writing the letter or report. This doesn't mean we should be blunt or tactless, just obvious. We spare the details until we have established our reason for writing. But we also get to the point clearly. We don't use obscure words or phrases that are familiar only to us or our organization. We state the purpose early; we don't bury it in the third paragraph somewhere between background detail and unimportant information. The reader should be able to tell at a glance what he's supposed to do, by the way.

"Will you send me five copies?"

"Wait until Friday—I'll call you then."

"Take the necessary steps to purchase the property."

All of this comes early and clearly in the report. Any supporting data comes at the end of the report or as an attachment to the letter.

Finally, here's a tip that's helpful in writing: to learn to write, *we must write*! We must practice, reread whatever we've written that didn't get the message across, then practice writing some more. We should read other people's writings and reports and analyze them. We should tear them apart, ask ourselves why they worded them as they did, admit to the good things they have done—*then imitate the good things.* Most good writers freely admit they started out by imitating those people who were already successful, so there's no shame in recognizing and copying good writing style. If there are people in the organization who have the reputation for good writing, study what they've written, see what it is that makes their material precise or easy to read, then try to do likewise.

## TIPS ON SPEAKING

One can't learn to speak well just by reading about it, but there are some things to look for and do that will improve our ability as speakers if we take advantage of the knowledge we've gained. All of the earlier suggestions we made about preparing obviously apply here, and how well we have done these things will determine much of the success or failure of our speech. But even the best preparation won't make competent speakers out of us. Above all, we must learn to *practice, practice, practice.* We don't have to practice every word we're going to say, but we need to work on phrases and try different combinations of words in order to get the most out of the words and phrases we use. Since we're more likely to be frightened at the beginning, we should practice our

opening remarks until they're as precise as we can make them. If we make a good start, the rest will come easier. Our confidence will be higher and the audience reception will be better. Another way to build our confidence is try out our ideas on other people. We shouldn't bore them or ask them to listen to the entire speech, but at least try to get them to react to our key points and ideas. Do they understand what we're trying to say? Do they see the logic we're using? Do they have some pretty good arguments for why we should say it differently?

When we start to speak, we must be alert to the audience's reaction. Do they look receptive? Are they bored? Is there anyone in the group that looks friendly and appears to be nodding agreement? (If so, it will build our confidence to direct our attention to him or her frequently to see how we're doing. Be careful, though; this person may not be a good gauge of the thinking and feeling of the entire audience.) One way to keep the audience with us is to get feedback from them. Look them in the eye when we've made a good point and try to get them to nod, smile, or frown. Don't be afraid to ask them to hold up their hands or even stand up if they are on one side or the other of an argument. This way we've made it clear that we're talking *to* and *with* them, not *at* them. And since we want to talk to them, we look at them, not the ceiling, the floor, or our notes. Look around the group; don't talk to just one side of the room, or to a few people on the front row.

There's nothing wrong with using notes—in fact, the audience expects it. But we need to use them well or not at all. Notes are just that: *notes*. They're not our speech written out. Very few people can get away with writing out their whole speech, then making it appear casual and natural. Certainly we can't do it if we are just beginning to learn to speak, so it's all the more important for us to make good use of our notes. But if our notes are not much shorter than the speech, then we're really just going to end up reading the speech. If so, then why not just send all the members of your audience a copy of the speech and save them some time? The rule for making notes is to put only the key points and phrases on them, plus any statistics or figures we need to remember. Again, practice will reduce the need for notes.

One thing that will help us eliminate the need for notes is to have some good speaking aids. Unfortunately, this introduces another dimension to our speaking and one that can also be misused. The trouble is that we tend to use things such as visuals, charts, chalkboards, or easels as crutches, rather than as aids. We depend on them to help *us,* not the audience. Just because we can get a lot of figures on a projected visual doesn't mean the audience is going to remember it all or even give it their attention for very long. There's nothing exciting about looking at a screen full of statistics for several minutes while a speaker reads and comments on them. If the aid doesn't make the point any clearer, don't use it. But some aids are vital. There's hardly any better way to show a relationship of parts to the whole than to use a pie chart or similar "whole" type of graph. Of course, we remember what we see much longer than what we hear, so good visuals are necessary to aid in retention. Also, visuals can save us a lot of words if we use them at the proper time and in the proper way. (It would take a lot of words to describe a cow, but a picture could get the message across in a hurry!) One important consideration is that if we decide to use a visual and think it will aid the audience in getting the message quickly and clearly, then we should make sure the audience can *see* the visual. The audience isn't likely to be very receptive when we say, "If you could see this, you'd note that it has two small holes."

## CONCLUSION

A final tip for those of us who find ourselves in the situation of having to write something or speak before a group of any size: *Be friendly on purpose.* Write and speak with a smile. Let our writing show we are friendly by our use of personal pronouns and people's names. Refer to things that the readers are familiar with rather than examples that relate only to our experience. The same is true for our speaking. Pleasantness is contagious. We can get away with a lot by saying it in a friendly way. This will come as we speak and write more and more, which is what we should do: speak and write more and more. To do our job well, we must steadily develop this side of it. There are many books written on the subject and many programs of self-help available. We need to take advantage of them as well as to practice by accepting every opportunity to write and speak that we get. If we do poorly, it's a sign that we need practice, not a signal to stop doing it altogether. If we do well, and we will if we keep trying, then we will be more likely to sell our ideas *and ourselves.*

## EXERCISES

1.  Individual activity: Each person in the group should write a memorandum to their boss about the activity they've been engaged in so far in the study of this book. It should be no longer than 50 words, and no more than two paragraphs. It may be edited and doesn't have to be copied over. When everyone is finished, they should be ready to read their memo to the rest of the group, or to others in the group.

2.  Small-group activity: Form subgroups of no more than four people. Let each person read their memo to the other members of their subgroup. Those members should look for unnecessarily long paragraphs, cumbersome, non-talk-sounding words, and traditional phrases. When all the memos have been read by their writers and comments made by the rest of the subgroup, each person should have at least five minutes to redo their memorandum.

3.  Individual activity: Let each person count up the number of words in the memo he or she wrote for exercise 1, then do the same for the memo written in exercise 2. Then have each subtract the smaller number from the larger. If the result shows that the second memo had *fewer* words than the first one, put a plus sign in front of the result, because that's a positive step forward. If it shows that the second memo had *more* words than the first, put a minus sign in front of the result, because that's a negative step backward. The idea is to see how many words have been *saved* in the rewriting. The whole group should read out their results so that a total for

the group can be obtained. (The object is to show that if these people can save this many words in writing only a 50-word memorandum, think what they'll do day after day in writing letters if they learn the lesson from this chapter!)

4. Group activity: Brainstorm a presentation that this group might make on how to save words and make the meanings clearer in their writing. This will be an oral presentation. Using the rules of good speaking, decide what the opening remarks should be, how attention can be obtained, and what illustrations should be included. The body of the speech should be outlined, showing the points to be made, and the suggested action should be close to the end. The conclusion should be emphatic and dramatic. It should actually be worked out, with the entire group developing a closing sentence for the speech. (While the speech probably won't be given, it's good material for someone who wants to pursue the subject further.)

# 14
# SELF DEVELOPMENT AND EVALUATION

It would be easy to stop the book at this point with just a few words of exhortation about personal growth and development. But new supervisors need to know how and where to develop themselves. As we get embroiled in the everyday problems of the job, we forget to look at ourselves to see if we are any better at what we're doing than we were a few months ago. In fact, we forget just what areas we are supposed to improve in. Little problems seem like big ones when they are with us, so we spend all of our time worrying about them and fail to realize that good supervisors have to think about the future as well as the present. Not only do we need to worry about the long-range objectives of the organization, but *we need to think about some long-range objectives for ourselves.* This isn't to say that we should spend all our time worrying about the next job or our "big promotion"; we simply have to realize that we really aren't going to be of much value to ourselves or the organization if we fail to grow to our full potential. But how do we develop ourselves and what are the areas that get first attention? The answers to these questions will make the difference in where we will be ten years from now and what we will be doing then.

## HOW DO WE DEVELOP?

How can we improve ourselves if we have all the problems of the job to worry about? The chances are that we are going to be so busy we can't take time out to train ourselves, or even do much planning about the future—*and here we have the first indicator that we need some development.* If we can't get the job done in the time allotted to us and still find some time to look to next week and next year, we may need to look at the way we are doing our job. Are we really organized in our work effort? Are we spinning our wheels doing things that should be delegated to others? Are we doing things over because we aren't doing them right the first time? Are we spending too much time on small, insignificant details, thereby letting problems get bigger and bigger? There are some pretty good signs to look for to see how well we are doing. Let's see what we can do about some of them.

First, consider the matter of not having enough time. One sign that we aren't utilizing our efforts very well is that we're working without taking time to plan. It's a vicious cycle, because the less time we have, the less we plan, and the less we plan, the more time it takes to do the job, so we run out of time. This goes on and on until finally we discover ourselves swamped with work and no time to plan it. The results are that we don't do a very efficient job of what we do, and may even overlook doing things that should be done. But how do we get out of such a dilemma? Well, one way is to turn the process around by stopping the cycle. We can start this by taking even five minutes at the start of the day to try to put things in order. If we don't do this, we'll probably do the first thing that comes up, whether it's important or not. Five minutes of deciding what needs to be handled first, and what can wait will save us from getting behind on important things. Another five minutes will allow us to decide what *we* need to handle and what *we can delegate* to someone else. Another tell-tale sign that we need to watch for in our supervisory job is the tendency to justify doing more and more of the job ourselves ". . . because I can do it in less time than it takes

to explain or train someone else." When we get into this cycle, we're doing more and our people are doing less. They're not happy because they see us doing work that they could and should be doing. We're unhappy because we're doing work we shouldn't be doing and may even decide that our people are lazy or have a poor attitude because they aren't doing more—*all because we haven't taken the time to plan our work very well.*

Remember, these are indicators we need to develop; they're not cures. The matter of how we develop is just as important. So far, we've seen that one way is to force ourselves to do five or ten minutes of planning and delegating. Another way is to give ourselves a little "instant success." We need confidence in ourselves and this comes from accomplishing something. Even if the thing isn't the biggest or most important job we've ever done, just finishing a task—and stopping long enough to take note of it—will boost our confidence a lot. How can we use this technique to our advantage? One simple method is to make a list of the things we have to accomplish in a period of time: a day, a week, or two weeks. (If our confidence is fairly low, a day works best.) We list the things on a page or two, and number them as they are listed. During the day we mark them off one at a time as we complete them. A good way to mark them off is with a transparent felt-tip pen. This way we can see what job we did, and that it has been accomplished. Seeing the broad strokes of the felt pen gives us a boost, because we see that as hectic as the job has been, we've still gotten a few things done. The next day, or at the end of the day, we make a new list, taking the things done off the list and adding new items for the upcoming day. Two things become pretty obvious as we follow this procedure: One is that it shows us how much we are really doing, and the other is that it gives us excellent chances for planning and organizing our work. As we see the things we have to do, we may see some duplication of effort. We may see that someone in the office can do two or three of the items because of the close relation between them. Also, as we list the things to be done, we have a chance to set some priorities. Naturally we want to do the important things first, so they should be near the top of the list. As we list the jobs, though, we often discover that we've missed some things that should be at the top of the list. If we hadn't made the list in the first place, we'd have missed something important or tried to do it in a hurry at the last minute, in either case doing less than what is expected of us. One caution here: Getting the right "size" is important. Writing down something that's going to take two or three days isn't going to give us much confidence; it will have just the opposite effect. If we see the list is short and each item takes a day or more, we need to list some of the parts of the job that can be done separately, and then cross these off as we accomplish them. This serves also to organize the large tasks into small, logical steps, helping us do a better job overall, and still giving us frequent "successes."

Another way we can develop is to watch others. First we watch our boss or someone else who is getting a lot of work done in the same time we're working. We study their behavior, their pattern, their organizing. We try to figure out what it is that makes them able to get as much done as they do. We can even discuss the subject with them. Don't make it a "flattery" session, though. They probably get a lot done because they make good use of their time; we don't want to be guilty of taking up too much of their time with our poor organizational habits. The way to discuss the subject is by asking the right questions, not by asking the person to solve our problems. We watch people work, then ask them why they did certain things. "Why did you call the meeting right at that time? What advantage did you gain by having the meeting at all?" Of course, we need to make it completely clear that we aren't questioning their wisdom, just trying to improve on our own. To improve on our perception, we can try to anticipate what their answers will be. We try to figure out the reasoning behind what was done, then see how close we are to the reasons they give. As we get closer and closer, we can see that our judgment is getting better. We're probably making better decisions on our own job now.

Next we make a conscious effort to judge the abilities of the people under us. We see how well they accept the responsibilities we give them, and make a conscious effort to give them more as they are able to handle them. We aren't trying just to get more work out of them; we're trying to expand their ability to handle more important assignments. Appraising others isn't the easiest thing to do; neither is delegating. Our ability to do these together, though, is one of the measures of success we can use. There are some who fear giving up responsibility and authority to those under them. Some fear that those under them will somehow get the credit and maybe even the job. Such lack of confidence in oneself is a sign of poor leadership and immaturity. One of the common traits of most good leaders is that they gather around themselves those who will assume responsibility when it is given. We should bear this in mind when we consider whether or not to let someone else do some of the work or make some of the decisions. Others fear giving up any responsibility and authority for an even less noble reason: They are afraid that if the job is done wrong, they will have to assume the blame. The truth is, that's the whole point—that we are willing to assume the blame in order to protect people under us and give them confidence to take the necessary risks until they have convinced themselves that they really can do well on the job. This doesn't mean that we are going to let them think that everything went well. It means that we will be a buffer between them and higher management. It means that we will know and tell them that they did the job well or poorly, but for a while at least they are safe under our protection. Once they feel this, they should respond with some good, creative decision-making. But if we don't create this kind of atmosphere, we will be stuck with the work ourselves and the problem we're talking about—not having enough time to do our job.

## THE NEXT JOB?

There are two reasons for developing ourselves—to do better in our present job, and to be ready for the next one. It is important to keep them in this order—the present job, *then* the next one. This may sound simple enough, but many good supervisors fail to get promoted because they get so interested in the next job that they forget to deal properly with the present one. We think, talk, and plan about the job we hope to get, letting the details of the present one slip. The first thing that happens is that our interest also begins to wane and pretty soon disaster strikes. An important assignment gets only meager attention. Details are overlooked and wrong decisions are made. Errors creep in and higher management gets involved in finding out what happened. And we, who were potentially able to take on more than we now have assigned, find that we're losing some of the work we used to have because someone up the line doubts our ability to handle even our present job. Some have said, "Do well on the present assignment, and the future will take care of itself." That's pretty good advice, except that it doesn't include all that's necessary to get ahead. It assumes that the things that are needed on the next job are already in the present one. This may not be true. If not, then it's well to develop in those areas where we are weak. If the next level above us requires considerable report writing and we don't think we're very good at it, this is one place we can start. We can look around for places to learn more about report writing, and we can look for opportunities to do some report writing on our present job. We can start off by making short reports on things the boss has asked about, then work up to longer and more complex ones. Just doing reports is a good way to learn, but we should do some studying and developing on the side so the experience will be meaningful. We follow the same routine in the other areas where we think the next job exceeds our present requirements. The advantage of this approach is that it will actually make us look better on our *present* assignment, rather than like we have abandoned any interest in it. While we are improving in our existing job, and improving our reputation at the same time, we are also preparing ourselves to take over a more responsible task when the opportunity arises.

One final word about the next job: let nature take its course; don't try to help it too much. Very few people can show where they have been successful at plotting their careers job-for-job. Most successful people will tell us that they got the job by being in the right place at the right time *and* by being ready when the occasion arose. It's not all luck, but luck surely plays a part. Our job is to be ready when the luck breaks for us. This means that we not only have developed ourselves to take over the added responsibility but also have covered the present one quite adequately. What this says, perhaps, is that in a real way *we help make our luck.* We need to remember that the ways to develop ourselves are too numerous to mention here. We could spend a lot of time just telling about the ways of growing through reading the right books and magazines. There are night schools and self-help courses. There are programs available within many organizations. But these are obvious to most of us, so we won't go into them here—not because they aren't good and profitable, but because they are the obvious things to do when we talk about self-development. We've tried to talk about some of the less obvious ones that can go along with these things. It might be said, and with accuracy, that part of the way of telling whether or not we are capable of taking on the next higher assignment is best determined by our ability to perceive the areas and ways of developing ourselves. Successful supervisors—new or old—will be sensitive to their own needs for development and will find ways of making the necessary improvements. Perhaps more important than that, they will see it as a challenge, not a chore. They will do it and call it fun, not exhaustive drudgery. Good supervision can be learned. If we take the time to back off and look at ourselves and where we are going, we'll see that we have already come a long way. It may have been hard work, but that wasn't all it was; there was probably a great deal of pleasure in making the trip. The rest of the way is even better!

## CONCLUSION

We've already said that appraising our people is a hard job. A much harder job is to *appraise ourselves.* Looking with objective eyes at our own strengths and weaknesses is close to impossible for most of us. One problem is that we know our *motives,* and when we know that they are good in a certain situation, even though we didn't perform too well, we tend to overlook our weaknesses in that situation. If we're going to improve ourselves, we'll have to be willing to see both the good and the bad in ourselves. We can't be too hard on ourselves—nor too easy. We look at things like time management, delegation, training, communication, interpersonal skills, etc., and imagine that we are appraising ourselves. We look for a standard, then put our *performance* against that standard—not our intentions. We also have another decision to make: Do we want to be better? That sounds like a ridiculous question, but many of us reach a plateau and decide—admitting it or not—that we really don't want to expend the effort or time to raise our performance level any higher. If we make this decision, we ought to be sure to keep it in mind and not end up somewhere down the line saying, "I could have had that better job if I'd wanted it," or "I wonder why the organization hasn't treated me better."

On the other hand, if we really are serious about being good supervisors—and that certainly represents anyone who has read this far in this book—we set some targets for ourselves, decide what must be overcome in order to reach them, and go about getting there. If we look at our-selves and decide that getting to a certain target is too far from our reach *at this time,* then we set another, short-range target and head for it. Also, if we decide that there are things in the way that aren't under our power to control, then we change our target. Notice that we've used the expression "target" often. We need a target to shoot at, a goal to strive for. It's more than saying, "I'd like to be a better com-municator some day." We have to be specific enough to say that "I'd like to be a better listener someday." We have to define the weaknesses that are keeping us from getting there, as well as defining the goal it-self. When we begin to get close to our goal, we have these decisions to make all over again, or we'll end up just drifting along, not getting any better nor any closer to any goal. There's a Hindu proverb that says, "If we don't know where we're going, any road will get us there." That's true of our self development. The idea is to set a target, then di-rect our energies toward getting there, remembering that the vast ma-jority of the successes we have aren't because of somebody else; they're because of us. We don't need "pull" from somebody else in the organi-zation to get ahead. We usually just need a little "push" from within ourselves.

## EXERCISES

1. Group activity: The entire group should brainstorm a list of things that should be considered in looking at oneself and evaluating pres-ent skills. What are the things that need to be looked at? (The list should be recorded, but heavily refined, so that it isn't too long and impossible to deal with.) Next, how can we determine what our future chances are for upward movement? What are the things we can look at in our own lives and our own jobs? The group should come up with a refined list of these things, too, and have it recorded for all the group to see.

2. Individual activity: Each person should look at the list of things about his or her present skills. Spend a few minutes using it and see how well it can be filled out. See whether it is really a usable list, or too nebulous to be meaningful. Spend some time on this before going on to the next exercise.

3. Group activity: Now that everyone has had a chance to use the list worked up in exercise 1, see what their reaction is. Brainstorm ways of refining it some more until everyone is happy that it will now give useful data.

4. Individual activity: Each person should now try to use the second list from exercise 1, the one dealing with things that need to be looked at in our lives and our jobs for determining the chances and direction of our future. Spend some time on this, trying to make it a meaningful activity, then go on to exercise 5.

5. Group activity: When everyone is finished with exercise 4, the group should evaluate the list as in exercise 3. Again the object is to refine the list down to a usable aid in determining where we are going and what it takes to get there. Each person should take both of these lists with them and review them at least once a year to measure their progress.

# EPILOGUE

Here we are at the end of another book on how to be a better supervisor. What have we learned? Only time will tell. What have we tried to offer? A supermarket designed to lay out the possibilities for growth and development. This is not to suggest that everything in the book is applicable to every new supervisor; the suggestions here are just that and no more—suggestions. The new supervisor will be no worse for having considered them; there is even the possibility that something that has been said will cause him or her to get a new idea, a new way of considering an existing problem. If the suggestion and the resulting idea pay off, then it won't take much more to justify the time it's taken to read the book.

The author repeats what has been said earlier: This isn't a rule book; it's a guide book. The ideas and suggestions have all been tried by someone at some time at some place with enough success to justify their being in this publication. Whether or not they work for you is not a measure of your effectiveness or your abilities—more likely it's proof that supervising people is complex and deserves all of our efforts and skills. If we are willing to put all our energies into the job, and are willing to learn the skills, then there can be only one result—we'll end up being good supervisors. There may be better rewards, but this one should suit most of us for a long time to come!

# INDEX